Trees and Shrubs of Mount Diablo

TEXT AND PHOTOGRAPHS BY
GLENN KEATOR

MOUNT DIABLO INTERPRETIVE ASSOCIATION

Trees and Shrubs of
Mount Diablo

ISBN 978-0-9748925-2-8

Printed in Korea by asianprinting.com

CONTENTS

PART 2. SHRUBS

ACKNOWLEDGMENTS

As always people have helped to make this a beautiful, informative, and useful book. The movers and shakers are the folks of Mount Diablo Interpretive Association, who have helped finance this project. Other matching funding came from the generous support of California State Parks Foundation.

I'd especially like to thank the following people: Rich McDrew for helping guide the project; Yulan Chang Tong for checking on the many plant details and names; Edith and Frank Valle-Riestra for careful and insightful editing; Cyndy Shafer, Environmental Scientist, and Karen Barrett, Interpretive Specialist, Diablo Vista District, for their comments on the final draft; and Rita Ter Sarkissoff for her beautiful layout and design.

If I have left anyone out, my apologies. Thank you all for a wonderful effort.

Glenn Keator, Berkeley, December 2007

INTRODUCTION

Trees and Shrubs of Mt. Diablo is an easy-to-carry guidebook for the beginning naturalist, amateur botanist, and nature lover who wants to know more about the environment around them. Although not intended to be comprehensive, it covers around ninety percent of the woody plants encountered on the Mountain.

Woody plants are generally subdivided into trees and shrubs. Trees are usually over fifteen feet tall and have one to four main trunks from which smaller limbs and branches depart. By contrast, shrubs are shorter and have many woody stems arising from their base. In this book, I'm including shrubs as low as one foot and trees over eighty feet high.

For convenience, the main body of the book is divided into a section on trees followed by a section on shrubs. For those plants that straddle the line between shrubs and trees, please check both sections.

The trees are further divided into the following categories:

- CONIFERS—trees with needlelike or scalelike leaves and seeds borne in cones.
- DECIDUOUS BROAD-LEAVED TREES—flowering or broadleaf trees that lose their leaves in fall and winter.
- EVERGREEN BROAD-LEAVED TREES—flowering or broadleaf trees that keep their leaves year round.

The shrubs are divided into the following sections:

- WOODY VINES—plants that climb.
- SHRUBS WITH COMPOUND LEAVES—the leaves are divided into two or more separate pieces.
- DECIDUOUS SHRUBS WITH SIMPLE LEAVES.
- EVERGREEN SHRUBS WITH SIMPLE LEAVES.

Within each of these sections of the book, the plants are arranged alphabetically by family, then alphabetically by common name. Each entry features a color photograph(s), the common name, the scientific name, the family, and paragraphs describing the plant. The photographs show a variety of aspects including the overall shape, leaf details, cones (for conifers), and flowers or fruits (for broad-leaved trees and shrubs). A mention is generally made of the distribution and plant communities where each species is found.

If by chance you know the name of a shrub or tree and want to learn more about it, look up the name in the index. While reading the description, you may sometimes come upon an unfamiliar word. Although I've tried to minimize technical language, certain scientific terms convey a meaning much better. If you don't know the meaning, turn to the glossary for a definition.

Before you look at the encyclopedia section, you may want to read about plant communities on the Mountain and about how plants are named.

PLANT COMMUNITIES
Shrubs and trees grow in predictable associations known as plant communities. Once you know these communities and the places where they occur, it's much easier to find a particular shrub or tree. Some species, of course, are found in more than one community. And some species are rare or appear only after fire. Here is a brief synopsis of the common communities.

OAK WOODLANDS
This classic community is found on gentle, rolling hills as well as in canyon bottoms throughout the Mountain. In some places, the oaks are widely spaced and create an open architecture. This aspect is often referred to as oak savannah. In other places, the oaks are denser and approach a forest

situation where the crowns are close together. Different species of oaks live in different sites: blue and interior live oaks *(Quercus douglasii* and *Q. wislizeni)* favor the more exposed sites; valley oak *(Q. lobata)* favors valley bottoms.

Where gray pine *(Pinus sabiniana)* and California buckeye *(Aesculus californica)* are mixed with oaks, the term foothill woodland is often used. Some of the steeper slopes on the Mountain feature fine examples of this variant.

• MIXED-EVERGREEN FOREST

This name is descriptive: a dense stand of trees that are (usually) evergreen. Only the deepest canyons and bases of north-facing slopes on the Mountain are protected enough from summer heat to support this forest (note that forests directly on the edge of streams are called riparian woodland).

Typical members of the mixed-evergreen forest include coast live oak *(Q. agrifolia)*, canyon live oak *(Q. chrysolepis)*, California bay *(Umbellularia californica)*, Coulter pine *(Pinus coulteri)*, and madrone *(Arbutus menziesii)*.

Good places to see this community are in limited parts of Mitchell Canyon and in the Pine Canyon area.

• RIPARIAN WOODLAND

Riparian woodlands are by definition restricted to permanent water courses and creeks. Because so much of the Mountain is wet only in winter and spring, these water courses are few. Good examples include Mitchell and Back canyons as well as adjacent Marsh Creek. The trees in this community grow tall, are deciduous, wind pollinated, and produce seeds that are mostly wind dispersed.

Typical trees of riparian woodlands include an upper story of Fremont cottonwood *(Populus fremontii)*, bigleaf maple *(Acer macrophyllum)*, white alder *(Alnus rhombifolia)*, and western sycamore *(Platanus racemosa)*. Shorter trees are mainly willows *(Salix spp.)* and sometimes blue elderberry *(Sambucus mexicana)*.

Riparian woodlands also are home to ropy vines of various sorts, and hedges of snowberry *(Symphoricarpos albus var. laevigatus)*, California rose *(Rosa californica)*, and sourberry *(Rhus trilobata)*.

KNOBCONE PINE FOREST

This forest is the most limited on the Mountain and is dominated by knobcone pine *(Pinus attenuata)*, which grows on shallow, rocky, nutrient-poor soils exposed to the full brunt of the hot, summer sun. Occasionally live oaks and a few other trees grow with the pine.

Knobcone pine has an unusual life cycle: it grows fast to maturity, produces abundant seed cones that fail to open, and releases its seeds only after fire, when it is also killed. The copious seeds germinate to re-establish the forest.

The only good example of this forest occurs in the Knobcone Point area of the Mountain.

CHAPARRAL

Chaparral consists of large, dense, impenetrable stands of (usually) evergreen shrubs. So dense are these stands, that a machete is necessary to pass through.

Chaparral grows on some of the steepest, rockiest slopes exposed to summer drought. The slopes usually face south or west; north-facing slopes, shaded in the afternoon, support oak and foothill woodlands.

Typical shrubs include vast stands of chamise *(Adenostoma fasciculatum)*, manzanitas *(Arctostaphylos spp.)*, wild lilacs *(Ceanothus spp.)*, and occasional other shrubs such as chaparral pea *(Pickeringia montana)*, mountain mahogany *(Cercocarpus betuloides)*, toyon *(Heteromeles arbutifolia)*, silk tassel bushes *(Garrya spp.)*, and scrub oaks *(Quercus spp.)*.

All shrubs feature tough leaves modified to cut down on excessive water loss during the long, hot summer days. Some have needlelike leaves, while others hold their leaves vertically, have a thick waxy cuticle, or are protected by dense mats of silvery or white hairs. Roots also probe deeply to reach hidden moisture.

Fire plays a dramatic role in the chaparral: although some shrubs are killed outright, many others stump sprout. While the original shrubs are regenerating, opportunistic, short-lived shrubs move in and make the most of the temporary gap in the vegetation. (Also in the first year following fire, many wildflower seeds germinate, bloom, and set seed.) Temporary components of the chaparral include yerba santa *(Eriodictyon californicum)*, pitcher sage *(Lepechinia calycina)*, golden fleece *(Ericameria arborescens)*, bush mallows *(Malacothamnus spp.)*, and golden eardrops *(Dicentra chrysantha)*, the latter a perennial wildflower.

• COASTAL SAGE SCRUB

On some of the poorest soils on the Mountain, a lower shrubby plant community known as coastal sage scrub predominates. Shrubs here are sometimes only three to four feet tall and have highly fragrant leaves that are partially shed during the summer drought.

The most common components of coastal sage scrub are black sage *(Salvia mellifera)* and California sagebrush *(Artemisia californica)*, but coyote bush *(Baccharis pilularis)*, yerba santa, bush monkeyflower *(Mimulus aurantiacus)*, and golden yarrow *(Eriophyllum confertiflorum)* are other frequent companions.

Coastal sage scrub sometimes merges with true chaparral—black sage is often seen in company with chamise, for example—or it invades the chaparral after fire.

HOW PLANTS ARE NAMED

What's in a name? A lot if you're dealing with plant names. Plants have two kinds of names: common names and scientific names. Why the dual system?

Common names are bestowed on well-known plants for a wide variety of reasons and often by more than one person. This means that a given plant may have several common names! Sometimes the names stick and enter everyday language; sometimes they don't. There are no rules guiding who gets to coin the names or how they enter into common currency. Multiple common names often happen where a species grows over a broad range. On the other hand, poorly known or inconspicuous plants have no widely recognized common name.

Although common names are sometimes descriptive and easy to remember, they may also be nonsensical, as in the case of elk-clover *(Aralia californica)*, a plant not remotely like a clover nor associated with elk.

For these reasons, common names are not as reliable as scientific names, which are stable and usually permanent: every species of plant has only one valid scientific name, which is understood throughout the world without ambiguity. The biggest obstacle to learning scientific names is that they're based on Latin or Greek and presented in a Latinized form. Fortunately for those of us who speak English, there are many Latin or Latin-derived words in our language. Thus, we have the advantage of recognition and recall of many of these names.

The more you decipher the meaning of the names, the easier it is to understand why the names were used and to remember them.

Consider the following examples of latin-derived names: *Pinus* for the genus we call pines, a cognate of our English word; *Lupinus* for lupines, a word meaning wolf and alluding to lupines' robbing soils of their nutrients. (In fact, lupines grow in poor soils because they have nitrogen-fixing nodules that help nourish them.) *Populus* is used for cottonwoods, a word related to our word *population* because a single cottonwood tree can create a grove of trees from its suckers.

CATEGORIES OF CLASSIFICATION

There are three categories that help identify plants and denote their classification. The first and largest category is family. All family names end in -aceae. Families usually contain several different genera, all of which share combinations of certain traits, which differ from all other families. Examples of tree and shrub families include Rosaceae (rose family), Pinaceae (pine family), Cupressaceae (cypress family)—all with names that sound and look like our English common names.

Not so intuitive are family names like Fagaceae (beech or oak family), Fabaceae (pea family), and Hippocastanaceae (horse-chestnut family). The Fagaceae's name is based on the Latin word for the beech tree, fagus; the Fabaceae is based on a member in the family called fava bean; and the Hippocastanaceae is from two Latin words—hippos for horse and castanea for chestnut.

Learning to recognize families simplifies plant identification. In the Mt. Diablo region, if you learn to recognize thirty to forty basic families, you'll be able to place over eighty-five percent of the plants in the correct family.

The next step in identification is to find the genus, a group of related species. Every scientific plant name starts with the genus name of the plant followed by its species designation. The species in each genus share many traits in common.

Common language often reflects the concept of genus; for example, *Quercus* contains most oaks; *Pinus* includes the pines; and *Rosa* covers the roses. Note that genus names are always either italicized or underlined and start with a capital letter.

All three of the genera mentioned above are large and contain many species (or, in common language, kinds). Examples of different species of oaks in our area include blue oak *(Quercus douglasii)*, valley oak *(Q. lobata)*, canyon live oak *(Q. chrysolepis)*, and coast live oak *(Q. agrifolia)*. Note that specific epithets always follow the genus name, are italicized or underlined, and start with a lower case letter.

In the examples given for oaks, the species designations have varying degrees of significance: *douglasii* honors David Douglas, who likely first discovered the blue oak; *lobata* alludes to the deep lobes of the leaves of valley oak; *chrysolepis*—golden scale—describes a gold powder found under the young leaves and on the acorn cups of canyon live oak; and *agrifolia* refers to the prickly teeth along the margins of coast live oak leaves.

For every entry in this book, I have given the most widely used common name(s) as well as the scientific names of the family, genus, and species. Genera and species that belong to the same family are described next to one another so that the reader can compare, for example, the different kinds of oaks and the different kinds of pines.

IDENTIFICATION GUIDE: PART 1. TREES

CONIFERS • Conifers are cone-bearing trees with needlelike or scalelike leaves. These trees never produce flowers; instead they bear two kinds of cones: tiny, ephemeral pollen cones that shed clouds of yellow pollen into the air, and substantial seed cones that contain one to many seeds. Seed cones may be fleshy and berrylike in the case of junipers or woody and hard in the case of pines. Pines are also noted for bearing their needles on minute spur shoots in a fixed number (two, three, four, or five in most cases).

Mt. Diablo is home to four different conifers, as follows:

CALIFORNIA JUNIPER *Juniperus californica*	Cypress family Cupressaceae

California juniper is a small, multitrunked tree or large shrub often spreading as wide as it grows tall. It is identified by its shreddy brown bark and tiny, bright green, scalelike leaves (use a good hand lens) that are highly fragrant when crushed.

Juniperus californica
CALIFORNIA JUNIPER, LOADED WITH SEED CONES

The trees are either male or female: the males produce minute yellow pollen cones in late summer or fall, the females make bluish, fleshy, berrylike seed cones an inch or so long. You can see the scales that make up these seed cones, especially when they're still young and greenish. Birds are attracted to these juniper "berries," nibbling on the fleshy scales and ingesting and later excreting the seeds.

California juniper is widespread on steep, rocky, sun-drenched slopes. Look for stands of it around Juniper Campground.

KNOBCONE PINE
Pinus attenuata

Pine family
Pinaceae

Pinus attenuata
KNOBCONE PINE, NEEDLES AND SEED CONES

Knobcone pine is fast-growing and starts life as a shapely and bushy tree with bright green needles in clusters of three on tiny spur shoots. As the trees age, they often become multitrunked and scraggly in appearance. The yellow pollen cones are borne in dense clusters between last year's needles and new buds that later make more needles. They open in midspring. The whorled seed cones develop early on this tree, often even on the trunk, and are retained for life. Each cone is four to five inches long, asymmetrical and pressed against the branches or trunk, and has knobbly scales on the outer side.

Knobcone pine belongs to a group referred to as serotinous or closed cone. Cones remain tightly closed after maturing even on the hottest days, opening to release their seeds only after fire or when a branch is broken. This mechanism allows knobcone pine to reforest a slope after fire. The trees grow quickly to maturity and seldom live more than fifty or sixty years.

Confined to nutrient poor, sandstone derived soils, knobcone pine is uncommon on Mt. Diablo. Knobcone Point supports an impressive stand of this unusual tree.

COULTER PINE   **Pine family**
Pinus coulteri   **Pinaceae**

Coulter pine is a heavy-trunked tree up to forty feet high with heavy limbs and branches. It bears long, thick, bushy, pale to gray-green needles in clusters of three on tiny spur shoots. The pollen cones develop in the same pattern and around the same time as they do on knobcone pine. Massive seed cones develop mostly near the top of the tree—each tapered, oval cone can weigh four or five pounds and reach over a foot in length. The sturdy, woody cone scales end in a stout, upturned spine. The scales bear large seeds that are edible to humans and animals alike. Because of the size of the seed cones, Coulter pines

Pinus coulteri
COULTER PINE, HABIT OF TREE

P. coulteri
COULTERI PINE, NEEDLES
AND SEED CONE

can be dangerous during a wind storm, when cones are torn loose.

Coulter pines are most widely distributed south of the Bay Area and are a common component of middle-elevation forests in the south Coast Ranges and mountains of Southern California. Their northern limit is Black Diamond Mines Regional Preserve near Antioch. A few stands are scattered on the more protected slopes near the base of Mt. Diablo. Good places to see them include Mitchell Canyon and the Coulter Pine Trail, which connects between Mitchell and Back canyons.

GRAY, FOOTHILL, OR GHOST PINE
Pinus sabiniana

**Pine family
Pinaceae**

Gray pine (formerly known as digger pine) has many characteristics in common with Coulter pine but differs in several easy-to-see ways. Gray pines are generally taller than broad and they are often two- or three-trunked just above ground level.

The long, grayish needles are borne in clusters of three on tiny spur shoots and are droopy, wispy, and sparse. (This is a pine whose foliage you can see through.) The pollen cones are much like the Coulter pine's and the seed cones, although almost as massive and heavy, are about as broad as long and only two-thirds the

Pinus sabiniana
GRAY PINE, TREES BACKLIT

length of Coulter cones. The tough, woody scales of the cones end in a substantial turned out spine. The seeds of gray pine are as large as Coulter's and are tasty and nutritious. Squirrels and jays avidly gather the seeds for food, planting them for later retrieval. California's Indians also considered these seeds excellent food.

Gray pine signals the hot, dry, inner foothill country of the Coast Ranges and Sierra Nevada. It often grows in company with blue oak (Quercus douglasii), interior live oak (Q. wislizeni), and California buckeye (Aesculus californica). It is widely scattered on the south-facing, rocky slopes of Mt. Diablo. Where gray and Coulter pines occur in the same area, as in Mitchell Canyon, the Coulter pines favor less exposed slopes where they lose water less rapidly than the drought-adapted gray pine.

DECIDUOUS BROADLEAF TREES • Unlike conifers, these trees bear neither needles nor scales. However inconspicuous they appear, their flowers ripen into seed pods and fruits. These ripened ovaries contain the seeds.

Broadleaf trees can be divided into deciduous species that lose their leaves in fall and winter or evergreen species that retain their leaves throughout the year. Although deciduous trees are obvious during the short days of the year, it is sometimes challenging to determine the durability of the leaves in spring and summer. As a general rule, deciduous leaves are thin and flimsy, while evergreen leaves are stiff, tough, and thick. It takes practice to make this determination so if you're just starting out, try looking at and feeling leaves of trees you already know.

Several species are found on Mt. Diablo, many of them along streams and other water courses.

BIGLEAF MAPLE
Acer macrophyllum

Maple family
Aceraceae

Bigleaf maple is a large tree with a broad, rounded canopy. The one to several trunks can reach sixty feet high with an almost equal or greater spread. The bark on mature trees is finely fissured and grayish brown.

Acer macrophyllum
BIGLEAF MAPLE, LEAFY CANOPY

The large (largest of any North American maple) leaves are rounded with several conspicuous and deeply indented palmate lobes. The young leaves are red in spring, are matte green in summer, and often turn golden yellow in fall before dropping.

The hanging chains of pale yellow flowers open just as the new leaves are emerging in early spring. Each small flower is provided with petals and nectar

A. macroplyllum
BIGLEAF MAPLE, FLOWERING BRANCHES

and are visited by bees. In fall, the ovaries ripen into pairs of winged samaras, which eventually turn brown as they're shed. Samaras spin on the wind like propellers, moving the seeds away from the parent tree to potential new homes. Bigleaf maple is always found by permanent water sources in the Bay Area. The trees only reach full size along streams with a year-round water table such as in Mitchell Canyon and along Marsh Creek on the east side of the Mountain.

BOX ELDER
Acer negundo

Maple family
Aceraceae

Despite its common name, box elder is a maple and is not related to elderberry. This fast-growing tree quickly reaches fifty to sixty feet high with an equal or somewhat lesser spread. The bark is similar to bigleaf maple but the leaves are quite different: instead of consisting of a single piece (simple leaves), each leaf is divided

Acer negundo
BOX ELDER, LEAVES

into three to seven narrow, coarsely toothed leaflets. The leaves are not as colorful as on bigleaf maple and turn a rather pale yellow-brown in fall before dropping.

Box elder is dioecious—there are separate male and female trees. In early spring, long tassels of dangling pinkish male flowers appear just before the new leaves emerge. Wind carries the pollen away. The female flowers are also borne in long *catkins* but are an inconspicuous green color and are seldom noticed until, in fall, they ripen into two-winged samaras similar in appearance to bigleaf

A. negundo
BOX ELDER, TRUNK AND
BARK PATTERN

maple. Wind moves the seeds to new homes just as it carries the pollen in spring.

CALIFORNIA BUCKEYE   Horse-chestnut family
Aesculus californica   Hippocastanaceae

California buckeye is a relatively short tree with a broad, rounded canopy and may reach twenty to thirty feet high. The bark is characteristically smooth and white to silvery gray, a beautiful sight in winter when

Aesculus californica
CALIFORNIA BUCKEYE IN
WINTER CONDITION

the branches are bare. The opposite leaves are round in outline but distinctively palmately compound; that is, each leaf is divided into several, elliptical, fingerlike segments. This is the only tree with such a leaf pattern.

A. californica
CALIFORNIA BUCKEYE,
CANDLE OF FLOWERS

After the leaves emerge in late winter, they turn apple green but it's some time before the flower candles mature and open—usually in May and June. Each upright candle consists of many, slightly irregular, fragrant, pale pink to white flowers. Look closely; only a few of those flowers have an ovary with a future seed since the mature seed pods are large and heavy and would otherwise overburden the branches that hold them. The leathery seed pods are pear-shaped and open by a slit to reveal a single, shiny, round, chestnut-shaped seed. Beware eating these seeds; they're highly toxic even though squirrels are immune to their poisons. Other parts of the tree are also poisonous, even the nectar is toxic to honey bees while native bees seem immune.

California buckeye is widely scattered on hillsides and near canyon bottoms (the seeds roll downhill). They often occur in the company of gray pine *(pinus sabiniana)* and various oaks *(Quercus* spp.*)*. They're found throughout California's foothills and are a common sight on Mt. Diablo.

WHITE ALDER
Alnus rhombifolia

Birch family
Betulaceae

White alder is a slender tree that soars to fifty feet high, often competing with other trees and vying for a place in the sun. The bark is pale and grayish white and the leaves are broadly elliptical, doubly toothed (fine and coarse teeth along the margins), and conspicuously veined. The leaves turn brown in autumn or sometimes are briefly pale yellow before dropping.

Alnus rhombifolia
WHITE ALDER, TRUNK AND
BRANCHES WITH NEW GROWTH

A. rhombifolia
WHITE ALDER,
LEAF DETAIL

White alder bears minute flowers in slender chains or *catkins*, which appear at winter's end. Both the male and female flowers occur on the same tree but are timed differently. First come the slender male catkins with their long yellow stamens that open to catch the wind. Later, the shorter, plumper, upright female catkins extend sticky stigmas to catch the pollen from a tree in its pollen-shedding stage. These female catkins ripen in late fall into short, brown, conelike structures (if you're familiar with coast redwood cones, alder catkins look similar). But appearances are deceiving: instead of scales with seeds as in true conifers, alder catkins are collections of woody bracts with tiny, winged samaras that are carried long distances on the wind.

White alder favors the same habitats as bigleaf maple—permanent water courses. Fine specimens are seen in Mitchell Canyon.

NORTHERN CALIFORNIA BLACK WALNUT
Juglans californica var. *hindsii*

Walnut family
Juglandaceae

Northern California black walnut is a somewhat slender tree to fifty feet high with deeply furrowed, dark brown bark and widely spreading roots that often send up suckers. The conspicuous leaves are

Juglans californica hindsii
NORTHERN BLACK WALNUT, BRANCHES SHOWING LEAVES AND YOUNG FRUITS

noticeably fragrant and pinnately compound (each leaf consists of several, broadly elliptical, toothed leaves arranged like the segments of a feather).

Inconspicuous, greenish flowers appear in spring as new leaves are emerging from their buds. The male flowers are in broad, dangling catkins with protruding stubby stamens. The female flowers are in small clusters at the base of the male catkins and open broad, sticky, crestlike stigmas at a different time to avoid self pollination. Later, the ovaries of these flowers ripen into nuts covered with a fleshy wrapping (technically, these fruits are called drupes and are similar to peaches and cherries). But the fleshy layer dries out and falls away revealing the inner nut with a hard shell and nutritious nutmeat (seed) inside. Black walnuts are difficult to crack without breaking the nutmeats and so are mainly used as the rootstock on which to graft the English walnut (*J. regia*).

J. californica hindsii
NORTHERN BLACK WALNUT, TREE TRUNK
AND CANOPY IN FALL

Northern California black walnut was probably originally uncommon in the wild. A few scattered groves occurred along permanent water courses in central California. One of these was in the Walnut Creek area so black walnut has always been native to Mt. Diablo. The distribution was greatly increased by the California Indians, who often carried the nuts to new sites, so that today this walnut is scattered throughout the inner Coast Ranges of central and northern California and the Sierra Nevada. Look for it in Mitchell Canyon and along Marsh Creek.

WESTERN SYCAMORE
Platanus racemosa

Plane tree family
Platanaceae

Western sycamore is a bold, multitrunked tree fifty feet high with an equal spread. Its limbs always seek a good source of light, so the trunks sometimes lean at precarious angles to achieve that goal. The bark is

Platanus racemosa
WESTERN SYCAMORE, NEW LEAVES
SHOWING STIPULES

a jigsaw puzzle of colors including white, buff, gray, and brown. (The bark changes color with age.) The oversized leaves resemble bigleaf maple in shape and design (they're palmately lobed) but are paler green, fuzzy when young, are borne singly (not in pairs), and have conspicuous, earlobe-shaped stipules at the base (no stipules on maple leaves). The leaves often turn fallow gold in fall.

The minute flowers of this tree are densely clustered into round balls that hang in chains below the leafy canopy. The male flowers produce wind-borne pollen while the female flowers—on the same tree—send out dark red, feathery stigmas to

P. racemosa
WESTERN SYCAMORE, TRUNK
AND BARK OF LARGE TREE

catch pollen. The clusters of female flowers ripen

into golf-ball-sized clusters containing many one-seeded fruits that break apart and are scattered by the winds.

Western sycamore is among our most distinctive riparian trees, following water courses often in company with bigleaf maple (*Acer macrophyllum*) and white alder (*Alnus rhombifolia*). Good places to seek it include Sycamore Canyon and Marsh Creek.

FREMONT COTTONWOOD
Populus fremontii

Willow family
Salicaceae

Fremont cottonwood is a substantial, tall tree to sixty feet or more high with a narrow, rounded crown. It often looks down over neighboring trees.

The grayish brown bark is deeply fissured and the bright green leaves are shaped like a broad triangle and are lined with coarse teeth. The leaves often flutter in the breeze because of their flattened petioles (leaf stalks).

Cottonwood is one more tree with inconspicuous, wind-pollinated flowers. The male trees bear hanging chains (catkins) of

Populus fremontii
FREMONT COTTONWOOD,
BRANCHES WITH LEAVES AND
SEED PODS SHEDDING
COTTONY SEEDS

clustered stamens; the female trees have similar chains of greenish flowers crowned by sticky stigmas that gather the pollen flying through the air. The seed pods ripen from late spring to early summer, shedding what look like wads of white cotton. Each tiny seed has a cluster of attached hairs for efficient, long-range wind dispersal.

Fremont cottonwood is one more tree that favors the edge of permanent water courses. As with many other riparian species, it reaches good development in Mitchell Canyon and along Marsh Creek.

BLUE OAK	Oak or beech family
Quercus douglasii	**Fagaceae**

No more characteristic group of trees grows on Mt. Diablo than the several, often difficult-to-distinguish oaks. Oaks occur in pure stands or are mixed with other broadleaf trees as well as gray pine (*Pinus sabiniana*).

Quercus douglasii
BLUE OAK LEAVES

Blue oak is a relatively small tree to thirty feet high with a broad, rounded crown. The pale, whitish bark is shallowly fissured or sometimes checkered. The two to three inch long leaves are narrowly elliptical, bluish in cast in summer and fall, and shallowly lobed. The combination of color and shallow lobes usually separates this oak from others.

Oaks are wind pollinated. In early spring, they send out long, dangling catkins of male flowers yellow from the large amounts of pollen produced by the stamens. By contrast, the minute female flowers are borne singly or in small clusters tucked into the angle between the new leaves and the stem. Each flower consists of a tiny ovary topped by three sticky stigmas that trap the wind-borne pollen.

From these, the acorns later develop and ripen in fall. The fat blue oak acorns sit in a warty cup.

Q. douglasii
BLUE OAK, TRUNK/BARK

Acorns provide food for numerous animals making oaks *keystone* species in their habitats. The Indians ground and leached the acorns as a major food source, although blue oak was not their favorite.

Blue oak is widely scattered in the foothills on rolling, dry slopes often in company with gray pine (*Pinus sabiniana*) and California buckeye (*Aesculus californica*).

GARRY OR OREGON WHITE OAK *Quercus garryana*	Oak or beech family Fagaceae

At first glance, Garry oak does not look much like valley oak because it's a smaller tree and its side branches are upright and often twisted. At closer

Quercus garryana
GARRY OAK, LEAFY BRANCHES IN FALL

view, though, the leaves and bark are similar. Garry oak leaves are the same basic shape as valley oak but the average size is somewhat shorter and the lobes generally fewer.

Although the flowers are almost indistinguishable from valley oak, the acorns provide a further means of separating these oaks. Garry oak acorns sit in a relatively shallow warty cup and the acorns themselves are almost as broad as they are long.

For us, Garry oak is an uncommon tree that appears in only a few places and usually in small numbers. Look for it near Rock City. This spotty distribution is probably because of the extremely hot, dry summers of our area; Garry oak becomes increasingly common as you go north into rainier Sonoma and Mendocino counties, where it often forms extensive woodlands.

CALIFORNIA BLACK OAK
Quercus kelloggii

Oak or beech family
Fagaceae

All of the other deciduous oaks belong to a subgroup of oaks known as white oaks; black oak stands apart and belongs to its own group. Black oak trees are often massive and multitrunked with deeply checkered, dark gray to black bark. The large leaves—up to seven or eight inches long—are deeply lobed, but

Quercus kelloggii
CALIFORNIA BLACK OAK, FALL LEAVES

each lobe ends in a bristlelike tip not present in our other oaks with lobed leaves. Black oak leaves are dramatic through the seasons: bright pink when they first emerge in spring and often golden yellow when they drop in fall.

The flower details are similar to other oaks

although the male catkins are often deep red in bud. The acorns are borne in a scaly cup and are about as broad as long. The oiliness of these acorns was appealing to the Indians, and this was arguably their

Q. kelloggii
CALIFORNIA BLACK OAK,
EARLY SPRING LEAVES

favorite food among the many different available oaks.

California black oak is never abundant on Mt. Diablo; look for it on protected, north-facing slopes and in canyon bottoms. A few trees are also seen in Rock City. It is more abundant in adjacent Morgan Territory Regional Preserve, where it often dominates the shadier, moister slopes.

VALLEY OAK	**Oak or beech family**
Quercus lobata	**Fagaceae**

No other oak in California matches the sheer size or spread of an old valley oak. Valley oaks have massive trunks with checkered, pale whitish bark and green leaves four to five inches long with several deep lobes. The branches of valley oaks display a characteristic drooping pattern, giving this oak a graceful presence wherever it occurs.

The details of the flowers are similar to blue and other oaks, and the flowers open in early spring just as the new

Quercus lobata
VALLEY OAK, TRUNK
AND BRANCHES

leaves are flushing out. The acorns that follow sit in a deep, warty cup and are longer than broad. Acorn characteristics are often most useful for identifying oaks but, unfortunately, they're only available for

Q. lobata
VALLEY OAK LEAVES

a limited time in the fall. They are avidly sought for food by a wide variety of mammals, birds, and insects.

Valley oak is predictable in its choice of environments: valley bottoms especially in well developed canyons with a high water table (although seldom with their roots directly in the water course). Mitchell, Donner, and Back canyons all feature valley oaks.

WILLOWS	Willow family
Salix spp.	Salicaceae

Willows are closely related to the cottonwoods but differ in several respects. In our area, for example, most willows are smaller trees, seldom exceeding thirty feet in height, and some more closely resemble overgrown shrubs and are thus multitrunked. Willows also feature narrow, usually lance-shaped leaves with or without teeth along their edges. Willow leaves may be green on both sides, grayish on both surfaces, or bicolored and paler underneath. Although willow bark sometimes resembles cottonwoods on old trees, the new twigs are often brightly colored in red, yellow, or orange-brown. These twigs are highly flexible and were extensively used to create the framework for the beautiful baskets made by the California Indians.

Willow flowers appear just as new leaves are emerging; the male trees feature stiff, upright, candlelike catkins with yellow stamens; the female trees feature similar catkins that are green and furnished with sticky stigmas. As with cottonwoods, willows are typically wind pollinated. The seed pods that ripen in summer are similar to cottonwoods and are filled with numerous, tiny, hair-covered seeds.

Salix **sp.**
WILLOW, MALE CATKINS
IN EARLY SPRING

There are several willows native to our region. Among them is arroyo willow (*S. lasiolepis*), a shrubby tree with brownish twigs and leaves that are usually hairy or whitish underneath and green on top. Red willow (*S. laevigata*) is a larger tree with red to yellowish twigs and leaf blades that are often highly glossy on the upper side and bearing a pair of tiny glands at the base of the blade. Shining willow (*S. lucida*) is a small tree with brownish twigs also featuring shining leaves but without the glands at the base of the leaf blade. Finally, narrow-leaved willow (*S. exigua*) is a multibranched shrub with linear leaves usually completely covered with silky, white hairs. The other willows have lance-shaped leaves.

As you can see, willows are not necessarily easy to sort out. Arroyo willow is the most widespread of the species found on the Mountain.

BLUE ELDERBERRY
Sambucus mexicana

Honeysuckle family
Caprifoliaceae

Blue elderberry is also considered a large shrub but old specimens may reach tree status, growing

Sambucus mexicana
BLUE ELDERBERRY, LEAFY BRANCHES
AND CLUSTERS OF RIPE FRUITS

up to twenty feet high with substantial trunks. The bark is dark brown and deeply fissured on mature specimens. The large leaves are borne in pairs, each leaf consisting of several elliptical, coarsely toothed leaflets arranged in a pinnate pattern. The crushed leaves have a somewhat odd and unpleasant smell and were used medicinally.

Blue elderberry produces a plethora of tiny, cream colored, fragrant flowers arranged in flat-topped

S. mexicana
BLUE ELDERBERRY, FLOWER CLUSTERS

clusters in May, June, or July depending on elevation. Although individually small, each flower produces abundant nectar with the result that the flowers are heavily visited by a wide variety of pollinators. Dull blue berries ripen in late summer, providing tempting morsels to many birds. They are also edible to humans and are used in making jellies and wine.

Look for blue elderberry near canyon bottoms

and along the cooler sides of north-facing slopes. It is widely distributed throughout Mt. Diablo and has a broad range through most of California. Its many Indian uses included twigs used to make flutes, clappers, and gambling sticks.

EVERGREEN BROADLEAF TREES • Evergreen broadleaf trees differ from the deciduous trees primarily by keeping their leaves through the entire year. (Actually, the oldest leaves on these trees are shed in the fall but there are always newer leaves retained on the branches to carry on.) In many cases, these two groups of trees are related; for example, there are deciduous as well as evergreen oaks.

As described above, the distinction between deciduous and evergreen is sometimes tricky to determine but generally evergreen trees have tougher, more durable leaves since they have to make do for more than a single year. All evergreen broadleaf trees bear true flowers and seed pods, but many, as in the case of the deciduous broadleaf trees, have tiny, wind-pollinated flowers. Only a few have obvious showy flowers.

| MADRONE | Heather family |
| *Arbutus menziesii* | Ericaceae |

Madrone is a dramatic, tall tree with a broad to oval crown. One of its most striking features is the smooth, orange-tan new bark, which in age curls and looks like wood shavings. Paddle-shaped leaves, six to eight inches long, are dark green on top, silvery beneath, and finely

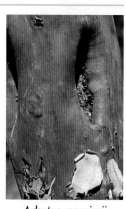

Arbutus menziesii
MADRONE, TRUNK/BARK

A. menziesii
MADRONE, FLOWERS

edged with tiny, sawlike teeth.

Nodding trusses of fragrant, white, lily-of-the-valley-like flowers appear in midspring. Warty, red-orange berries ripen in fall and attract birds.

Madrone is widely scattered in the cooler mixed-evergreen forests on north-facing slopes and in canyon bottoms but it is nowhere abundant on Mt. Diablo. Look for it in the Castle Rock and Rock City areas.

BLUE GUM	**Myrtle family**
Eucalyptus globulus	**Myrtaceae**

Blue gum is often referred to simply as eucalyptus, but in fact it is only one of several hundred species native to Australia. Introduced in the late 1800s, it has been widely planted and now grows on its own in many sites.

Eucalyptus globulus
BLUE GUM, JUVENILE LEAVES
SHOWING BLUE POWDER

These fast-growing trees may top 100 feet high and bear a narrow crown; sickle-shaped, highly fragrant mature leaves; and long strips of peeling tan gray bark. When young, the juvenile foliage consists of pairs of elliptical leaves covered with a bluish powder, which gives rise to the common name.

The white flowers

of blue gum hang in trusses below the leaves, and appear in summer. Each flower consists of a cap which pops off as the buds open, and numerous white stamens that attract pollinators. The "gum nuts" that follow are inverted woody vases with a second cap that eventually drops off to allow the seeds to be shaken out.

Blue gum is mainly found near dwellings and other occupied sites in the Mt. Diablo region and throughout most of foothill California.

COAST LIVE OAK	Oak or beech family
Quercus agrifolia	Fagaceae

Coast live oak (and all other so-called live oaks) differ from blue, valley, and black oaks in being evergreen. The broadly spreading, rounded crown is a signature feature of this oak. Its dark green leaves have curled-under margins that are lined with small,

Quercus agrifolia
COAST LIVE OAK, CANOPY

prickly teeth. The massive trunks feature dark gray bark that in age develops deep fissures. (Coast live oak belongs to the black oak group and sometimes hybridizes with the California black oak.)

As with other oaks, the male flowers are dangling, wind-pollinated catkins that appear in early spring, while the minute female flowers are borne in small

Q. agrifolia
COAST LIVE OAK,
STOUT TRUNKS

groups at the base of new leaves on the current year's growth. Coast live oak acorns sit in a shallow, scaly cup, and are broad and plump in appearance. Like other oaks, these acorns contain highly nutritious food, consisting of

Q. agrifolia
COAST LIVE OAK,
DETAIL OF YOUNG LEAVES

starches, fats, and proteins protected from direct human consumption by bitter tannins (the acorns have to be leached first to be edible).

Coast live oak flourishes best on coastal hills; in the Mt. Diablo area it seeks the higher water table and partial shade of canyon bottoms. Look for it in Donner and Mitchell canyons.

GOLDCUP OR CANYON LIVE OAK *Quercus chrysolepis*	Oak or beech family Fagaceae

Canyon live oak has a variable crown according to whether it is competing for light among other trees or stands by itself. The leaves either bear prickly, hollylike teeth or are smooth margined. The prickly kind are most often confined to the lower branches, where they deter deer from browsing them. The undersides are dramatically different from other oaks—they're pale gold when young, later turning a whitish blue-green color. The tops of these leaves are dark green like most other evergreen oaks.

Quercus chrysolepis
CANYON LIVE OAK,
NEW SPRING LEAVES

The male catkins and young female flowers are like other oaks. The acorns ripen in a warty cup covered with gold powder (hence the name, goldcup oak) and are fat and rounded.

Q. chrysolepis
CANYON LIVE OAK,
ACORN AND ACORN CUP

Canyon live oak is common mostly on the north-facing slopes of Mt. Diablo despite the common name. Dwarf forms of this oak grow in company with the interior live oak along part of the Mary Bowerman Trail (formerly named the Fire Interpretive Trail) just below the summit of the Mountain.

INTERIOR LIVE OAK
Quercus wislizeni

Oak or beech family
Fagaceae

Interior live oak is a sister species to the coast live oak and generally replaces it in the inner, hot, summer-dry foothills. The two share a generally similar crown and outline and similar dark gray bark but interior live oak trees are seldom as

Quercus wislizenii
INTERIOR LIVE OAK, BRANCHES
LADEN WITH MALE CATKINS

massive or as tall as coast live oak. The leaves vary—
some have prickly margins, especially on the lower
branches, while others are smooth edged. But unlike

the canyon
live oak,
whose leaves
are similarly
variable,
interior live
oak's leaves
are green on
both sides.
And the

Q. wislizenii
INTERIOR LIVE OAK LEAVES

leaves lie flat without curled edges unlike the coast
live oak.

The male catkins and female flowers are similar
to other oaks, and the ripe acorns sit in a scaly cup,
and are generally long and pointed.

Interior live oak prefers dry, steep hillsides, where
it sometimes joins blue oak (*Q. douglasii*). It also
occurs near the top of Mount Diablo on rocky
soils. You can see it, for example, along the Mary
Bowerman Trail near the mountain's summit.

CALIFORNIA BAY OR BAY-LAUREL	Laurel family

**CALIFORNIA BAY
OR BAY-LAUREL**
Umbellularia californica

**Laurel family
Lauraceae**

California bay is somewhat
of a chameleon of a tree
now with a broad rounded
crown, now with a narrow,
soaring crown, now
stunted and wind pruned,
all according to growing
conditions. It often sports
multiple trunks with fine,

Umbellularia californica
CALIFORNIA BAY, FLOWERS

shallowly checkered, dark
brown-gray bark. The

lance-shaped leaves are highly fragrant, especially on hot summer days, when their odor may be overpowering. These leaves have a scent similar to the European bay (*Laurus nobilis*) used to flavor food, but one should exercise caution in using

U. californica
CALIFORNIA BAY, YOUNG FRUITS

our own bay leaves for that purpose because of their potency.

California bay blooms in winter or very early spring with umbel-like clusters of small, pale yellow flowers loaded with nectar. These blossoms often provide the only source of nectar to winter-foraging bees and other insects. The fruits that follow look like miniature, speckled

U. californica
CALIFORNIA BAY,
FLOWERING BRANCHES

green avocados but eventually turn dark purple in the fall when ripe. Some rodents are fond of the flesh of these fruits; Indians roasted and ground the single large seed as a condiment.

California bay is a common component of mixed-evergreen and oak woodlands throughout most of the Mountain. It grows in reduced size near the summit.

PART 2. SHRUBS

No hard and fast rule separates trees from shrubs. Shrubs are generally shorter than trees and, in place of having one to several massive trunks, shrubs have many smaller branches arising from their roots to form a bush.

I have subdivided the many kinds of shrubs into the following categories for convenience:

- VINES. Only woody vines are included; herbaceous vines like manroot (*Marah* spp.) and wild sweetpea (*Lathyrus vestitus*) are not described.

- SHRUBS WITH COMPOUND LEAVES. These shrubs have leaves that consist of more than one piece; each leaf is divided into two or more separate leaflets.

- SHRUBS WITH SIMPLE, DECIDUOUS LEAVES. These shrubs feature leaves of one piece which may be lobed, toothed, or wavy. Their leaves drop in fall to leave bare branches in winter.

- SHRUBS WITH SIMPLE, EVERGREEN LEAVES. These shrubs keep some of their leaves throughout the year.

VINES • Vines are climbing plants unable to support themselves. Although their roots are anchored in the soil, their stems wind around other shrubs or trees and help support their leaves in the sun. All local species are winter deciduous.

CHAPARRAL CLEMATIS OR VIRGIN'S BOWER
Clematis lasiantha

**Buttercup family
Ranunculaceae**

Virgin's bower is a woody vine growing to over thirty feet long in order to climb high in tree and shrub canopies. Some shrubs may eventually be so completely covered by a clematis bower that their leaves are all but hidden. The ropy stems feature long strips of shreddy bark, and the compound leaves are arranged in pairs along the stems. The leaf stalks twist around other plants to help support the stem as it climbs.

Clematis lasiantha
CHAPARRAL CLEMATIS,
MASSES OF FLOWERS

The clusters of creamy, star-shaped flowers are showy and open in midspring. After the flowers fade, the fruits ripen into equally showy "poofs" of white, fuzzy seed heads that break apart and are carried away on the wind. Each fruit consists of a small, narrow pod tipped by a long, plumelike white style.

Virgin's bower is common throughout the Mountain and is especially characteristic of the chaparral plant community, where it often grows on such shrubs as toyon (*Heteromeles arbutifolia*) and wild lilacs (*Ceanothus* spp.).

ROPEVINE, PIPEVINE, OR RIPARIAN CLEMATIS
Clematis ligusticifolia

Buttercup family
Ranunculaceae

Ropevine closely resembles the virgin's bower but its stems may reach higher into the canopy, often ascending into the crowns of such riparian

trees as Fremont cottonwood (*Populus fremontii*) and bigleaf maple (*Acer macrophyllum*).

Clematis ligusticifolia
RIPARIAN CLEMATIS, VINE IN FLOWER

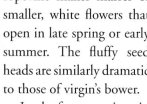

C. ligusticifolia
RIPARIAN CLEMATIS, YOUNG FRUITS

Both species have similar leaves and fruits, but ropevine makes masses of smaller, white flowers that open in late spring or early summer. The fluffy seed heads are similarly dramatic to those of virgin's bower.

Look for ropevine in canyon bottoms with permanent streams or with a high water table. Mitchell Canyon is an excellent place to see it.

VINE HONEYSUCKLE
Lonicera hispidula

Honeysuckle family
Caprifoliaceae

Vine honeysuckle grows into great, ropy trusses which in age look like the tropical lianas that supported Tarzan. It features pairs of oval, pale green leaves attached directly to the stems. The leaves are covered underneath with stiff hairs (use a good hand lens) and are fused together to form a broad disc around the stem just below the flower clusters.

Vine honeysuckle bears racemes of two-lipped, pale pink (occasionally white) flowers. Don't be disappointed when you smell them—they have little odor, while many of the popular cultivated garden honeysuckles are highly fragrant. Translucent red berries, insipid to humans but attractive to birds, ripen in the fall.

Lonicera hispidula
VINE HONEYSUCKLE, VINES IN FRUIT WITH BRIGHT RED BERRIES

Vine honeysuckle is widely distributed on the Mountain in woodlands and forests.

HIMALAYAN BLACKBERRY
Rubus discolor

Rose family
Rosaceae

Himalayan blackberry is most often referred to simply as "wild" blackberry despite the fact that it is not at all native but comes from Asia. Even more aggressive than the dewberry, Himalayan blackberry is easily told by its coarse stems that bear seriously vicious prickles, and its even larger leaves that are divided fanwise into five stout leaflets. The flowers are also larger than dewberry's and white to pale pink. Large, delicious berries ripen in the summer.

Fortunately, Himalayan blackberry has not invaded most of the natural habitats on Mount Diablo but it can be sought in canyons, often near streams and in partial shade. It is far more abundant in coastal areas, where fog is prevalent.

DEWBERRY OR CALIFORNIA BLACKBERRY
Rubus ursinus

Rose family
Rosaceae

Dewberry is a fast-spreading, scrambling plant with stems lined with slender prickles; coarse

leaves divided into three, toothed leaflets (trifoliate); and clusters of small, white flowers resembling single roses. The miniature blackberries that

Rubus ursinus
NATIVE BLACKBERRY, VINES IN FLOWER

ripen in summer are tasty and attractive to a wide range of animals.

Dewberry is common in shaded woods and along streams throughout much of the Mountain and is widely distributed through California's foothills.

CALIFORNIA WILD GRAPE
Vitis californica

Grape family
Vitaceae

California wild grape is an exuberant vine that often grows into the crown of trees along water courses. It

features broad, rounded, coarsely toothed leaves and curled tendrils that help it cling as it climbs. The tiny, yellow-green flowers are borne in dense clusters and appear in late spring. Small, purple grapes

Vitis californica
CALIFORNIA GRAPE, YOUNG
LEAVES AND FLOWER BUDS

ripen in fall. Although seedy, the fruits are edible and attractive to wildlife. California wild grape finishes the season in November, when its leaves turn shades of luminous yellow and red before dropping.

Look for California wild grape in well-watered canyons such as Mitchell Canyon where it often forms dense draperies.

SHRUBS WITH COMPOUND LEAVES • For the beginner, compound leaves often pose a problem: How do you know if a leaf is compound or simple? There are several clues. First, look for a bud just above where the leaf is attached to the stem—leaflets of a compound leaf do not have buds at their base but the whole leaf does. Second, some leaves have a pair of tiny, green appendages at their base (stipules) but leaflets never do. Third, leaflets of compound leaves lie flat all in the same plane whereas the leaves on a stem seldom do.

Some of the most distinctive shrubs on Mount Diablo feature various forms of compound leaves. When the leaflets are arranged along a long stalk like the parts of a feather, the leaves are pinnately compound. If, by contrast, the leaflets are arranged like the fingers on a hand, they're palmately compound. Several shrubs have only three leaflets per leaf, in which case they're trifoliate.

CALIFORNIA SAGEBRUSH
Artemisia californica

Daisy or composite family Asteraceae

California sagebrush is a shrub to four or five feet high with semievergreen, grayish leaves deeply slashed into many linear divisions to give a feathery appearance. (The leaves are semievergreen because in dry summers, they're partially shed.) These leaves are highly fragrant and smell like sage. The tiny heads of yellow-green flowers appear in slender clusters in fall but often go unnoticed.

California sagebrush is frequent in open oak

woodlands and as a component in coastal sage scrub, which sometimes replaces chaparral. It is found throughout the Mountain.

Artemisia californica
CALIFORNIA SAGEBRUSH, BRANCHES

CALIFORNIA BARBERRY
Berberis pinnata

Barberry family
Berberidaceae

California barberry is a stiffly branched, colonizing shrub to eight feet high with a bright yellow inner

bark and evergreen, pinnately compound leaves. The leaflets resemble prickly holly leaves (sometimes the common name *holly grape* is used). The dense trusses of yellow flowers appear in late spring and are followed by grapelike, pale blue berries that are edible but sour.

Berberis pinnata
CALIFORNIA BARBERRY,
LEAVES AND FLOWERS

California barberry is occasional on Mt. Diablo, where it usually grows in dense woods. It is much commoner on rocky hills overlooking the immediate coast.

BROOMS
Cytisus scoparius,
Genista monspessulana,
and Spartium junceum

Pea family
Fabaceae

The several brooms are all green-twigged shrubs with dense bunches of broomlike branches that produce colorful masses of bright yellow, sweet-pea-like flowers. Details of the leaves and twigs vary: *G. monspessulana* (French broom) has three obvious leaflets per leaf; *C. scoparius* (Scotch broom) generally has simple leaves (occasionally divided into threes); and *S. junceum* (Spanish broom) has minute or no obvious leaves. Spanish broom features the largest and showiest flowers of the three.

Cytisus monspessulanus
FRENCH BROOM,
FLOWERING SHRUB

None of these brooms is native; all come from parts of southern Europe and the Mediterranean region. Introduced to horticulture for their attractive blossoms, many have escaped into the wild to become serious pests that crowd out many kinds of native plants. Thankfully, brooms have not become a major issue on most of the Mountain; the dry summer climate precludes their rapid spread. Their greatest inroads have been in forests in the Sierra foothills and in

FLOWERING ASH	Olive family
Fraxinus dipetala	Oleaceae

Flowering ash is a large, openly branched, deciduous shrub to fifteen feet high with pinnately compound leaves consisting of three to seven rounded leaflets. Nodding trusses of small white flowers appear in midspring. Each flower is unusual in bearing only two petals, an unsual number when most shrubs have four- or five-petaled flowers. And it differs from its relatives (Oregon and Fresno ashes), which are petal-less and wind pollinated. Singly winged fruits

(samaras) ripen by summer's end and go fluttering off on breezes.

Flowering ash is relatively uncommon on Mt. Diablo. Look for it along the Donner Canyon Road.
coastal mountains.

Fraxinus dipetala
FLOWERING ASH,
LEAVES AND TRUSSES
OF FLOWERS

DEERBROOM LOTUS
Lotus scoparius

Pea family
Fabaceae

Deerbroom lotus is a subshrub: a bushy plant that is woody only at the base. As its name suggests, it forms broomlike clusters of greenish stems that

Lotus scoparius
DEERBROOM LOTUS,
FLOWERING BRANCHES

grow to around two feet high. After winter rains, the stems are covered with small, lopsided, pinnately compound leaves, which often drop during summer drought. Short racemes of bright yellow, sweet-pea-shaped flowers appear in mid to late spring. Tiny, pea-pod-like fruits ripen in summer.

Deerbroom is a common component of coastal sage scrub and chaparral, often flourishing in places where larger shrubs don't dominate, such as along road- and trailsides. It is found throughout Mt. Diablo.

SILVERLEAF OR BLUE BUSH LUPINE
Lupinus albifrons

Pea family
Fabaceae

Of the several different lupines native to Mt. Diablo, only silverleaf lupine is a shrub. Normally it grows three to four feet high with an equal spread and features distinctive, semievergreen, silvery, palmately compound leaves. The silver color comes from

Lupinus albifrons
SILVER-LEAF LUPINE IN FULL FLOWER; CALIFORNIA SAGEBRUSH IN FRONT

numerous whitish hairs that are pressed against the leaves to reduce water loss (use a good hand lens). Spikes of fragrant, blue-purple flowers emerge in early spring and are strong draws to bees.

Silverleaf lupine is a common component of coastal sage scrub, chaparral, and open oak woodlands throughout the Mountain. It is one of the delightful companions to the spring hiker, favoring rocky trailsides.

CHAPARRAL PEA
Pickeringia montana

Pea family
Fabaceae

Chaparral pea is a stout, rigid shrub to eight feet high with thorny side branches and small, evergreen, trifoliate leaves. Rather drab out of flower, it

Pickeringia montana
CHAPARRAL PEA, FLOWERING BRANCHES

is transformed in late spring by masses of showy, magenta-pink, sweet-pea-shaped flowers. Tiny pealike pods follow.

Chaparral pea is widely scattered in the chaparral, especially on rocky slopes in the upper part of Mt. Diablo. Its roots sucker to produce colonies wherever it grows.

HOPBUSH	Rue or Citrus family
Ptelea crenulata	Rutaceae

Hopbush grows as a large shrub to fifteen feet high. It features purplish new bark; broad, trifoliate leaves imbued with a bitter ruelike odor; and clusters

of small, cream colored, star-shaped flowers in midspring. Unusual round fruits are encircled by a wing for wind dispersal in fall.

Ptelea crenulata
HOPBUSH, LEAVES AND FLOWERS

Hopbush is generally uncommon in most parts of California but not on Mt. Diablo, where it favors north-facing slopes in chaparral and open woodlands. It is abundant along the trail from Mitchell Canyon to Deer Flat.

SQUAWBUSH OR SOURBERRY	Sumac or cashew family
Rhus trilobata	Anacardiaceae

Squawbush makes loose hedges of gracefully arching branches to six feet high, colonizing ground in favorable habitats. The bark and leaves carry a strong astringent odor that is obvious on warm days. Although the trifoliate leaves look suspiciously similar to poison oak, the pattern of the leaflets is different (as is also the branch pattern). Close clusters of small, pale yellow flowers in mid to late spring settle the question of identity beyond all doubt. The flowers are followed by sticky red berries that ripen in late summer or early fall.

Rhus trilobata
SQUAWBUSH
IN FRUIT

Look for squawbush in well-watered canyons in partial shade. Mitchell Canyon is home to several colonies, some of which grow next to their cousin, the poison oak (*Toxicodendron diversilobum*).

CALIFORNIA ROSE
Rosa californica

Rose family
Rosaceae

California rose forms loose hedges along streambanks, where it grows vigorously to six feet high. Its stems are armed with stout, recurved prickles. The pinnately compound leaves look like garden roses and are shed in fall. Open clusters of fragrant, pale pink, roselike flowers open from late spring through summer. The fruits are bright red-orange "hips" that ripen in

Rosa californica
CALIFORNIA WILD ROSE,
CLUSTER OF FLOWERS

fall and attract birds. Rose hips are actually fleshy cups that surround the dry, one-seeded fruits contained inside.

California rose is widespread along streams and canyon bottoms with a high water table. It is typical of riparian woodlands such as Mitchell Canyon.

WOOD ROSE
Rosa gymnocarpa

Rose family
Rosaceae

Wood rose looks like a miniature version of California rose, forming loose hedges up to four

feet high with slender stems; slender, straight prickles; and miniature, pinnately compound, roselike leaves. The small pale to dark pink flowers are also in scale with the rest of the plant and are sparsely produced in late spring. Small orange rose hips follow. An unusual feature of this particular rose is that the hips lack the usual crown of sepals seen in other roses.

Rosa gymnocarpa
WOOD ROSE,
SHRUB WITH FLOWERS

Wood rose is frequent in mixed-evergreen forest and oak woodlands throughout the Mountain.

POISON OAK
Toxicodendron diversilobum

Sumac or cashew family
Anacardiaceae

Poison oak is the most infamous shrub on Mt. Diablo. It may grow as a low, woody ground

cover, as a large shrub, or as a woody vine that climbs high into tree canopies in the shade. This deciduous shrub is dangerous at all times of the

Toxicodendron diversilobum
POISON OAK,
FLOWERING BRANCH

year because of the irritating urushiol found in its stems and leaves. The twigs are stiff, brownish, and upright with stubby side branches. The trifoliate

T. diversilobum
POISON OAK,
SHRUBS LEAFING OUT IN EARLY SPRING

leaves are variously lobed, red when they first open in spring, and red again in the fall before dropping. The tiny white flowers are borne in hanging chains and are delightfully fragrant (you can't get a rash from the odor). Dull white berries ripen in summer and are sought by birds.

Sadly, most trails on the Mountain have poison oak. This shrub is common in woodlands, forests, chaparral, and coastal sage scrub. Special care should be exercised to learn to avoid it in its leafless winter condition.

DECIDUOUS SHRUBS WITH SIMPLE LEAVES

Although a large number of the native trees on Mt. Diablo are deciduous, a somewhat smaller proportion of the shrubs are. This is perhaps because many shrubs live in the chaparral plant community, which is well represented on many slopes of the Mountain. Most of the shrubs there are evergreen, not deciduous.

Most of our deciduous shrubs, by contrast, live in woodlands and in canyons, in habitat that dries out more slowly.

CALIFORNIA BRICKEL BUSH
Brickellia californica

Daisy or composite family
Asteraceae

California brickel bush often goes unnoticed because of its unshowy flowers. It is a modest bush to four or five feet high with soft, gray-green, fragrant, triangular leaves. The tiny, greenish white flower

Brickellia californica
CALIFORNIA BRICKEL BUSH, NEW LEAVES

heads appear in late summer or early fall and although not showy, release a sweet fragrance into the evening air to attract pollinators. The flowers are followed by tiny, one-seeded fruits that are carried away on breezes by attached white hairs.

California brickel bush is widely scattered on the Mountain. Look for it along the sides of canyons such as Back Canyon or amongst coastal sage shrubs on semishaded slopes.

MOUNTAIN MAHOGANY
Cercocarpus betuloides

Rose family
Rosaceae

Mountain mahogany is a large shrub to fifteen feet high with rigid, stiff branches; grayish bark; and small, semideciduous, elliptical leaves lined with coarse teeth and carrying an imprinted, pinnate vein pattern. Masses of small, cream colored, petalless flowers appear in midspring but the real show comes in summer when the single-seeded fruits carry long, plumed, white styles. A shrub in full fruit looks like it's covered with hundreds of tiny, white candles.

Mountain mahogany is widely scattered in the chaparral on steep, rocky slopes and is unusual in being winter deciduous.

Cercocarpus betuloides
MOUNTAIN MAHOGANY,
FLOWERS AND LEAVES

DESERT OLIVE
Forestiera pubescens

Olive family
Oleaceae

Desert olive is an intricately branched shrub to eight feet high, sometimes with thorny side branches. The small, narrowly elliptical leaves have an especially bright green hue and are borne in dense clusters. Tiny, fragrant, clustered green flowers attract bees to their nectar in early spring as the new leaves appear. Small, dark purple, olivelike fruits follow in summer. Although these fruits are suggestive of the cultivated olive (*Olea europea*), they contain no oil but are attractive to birds.

Forestiera pubescens
DESERT OLIVE,
TRUNK AND BRANCHES

Desert olive is a seldom-encountered shrub that follows stream banks in woodlands. You can see it on Mt. Zion and on Mangini Ranch but its main range is to the south in the south Coast Ranges, arid Southern California mountains, and the margins of deserts.

CREAMBUSH OR OCEAN SPRAY
Holodiscus discolor

Rose family
Rosaceae

Creambush is a shrub with loosely flowing, often arched branches to around ten feet high. Although

Holodiscus discolor
CREAMBUSH/OCEAN SPRAY
SHRUB IN FLOWER

the overall leaf pattern resembles the mountain mahogany, creambush leaves are soft, velvety, and pleasantly fragrant with a hint of fruitiness. The dense panicles of tiny white flowers (pink in bud) are carried beyond the leaves and open in summer. They ripen into one-seeded, dark brown fruits that remain on the shrub even when the leaves have dropped in fall.

Creambush is common in oak woodland and mixed-evergreen forest throughout the Mountain.

OSO BERRY
Oemleria cerasiformis

Rose family
Rosaceae

Oemleria cerasiformis
OSO BERRY,
FLOWERING SHRUB

Oso berry is named for its fruits which are attractive to many kinds of wildlife, including bears (oso = bear in Spanish). The shrubs are openly branched to eight feet high with broadly elliptical leaves that briefly turn yellow in fall. Hanging trusses of small, white, apple-blossom-like flowers appear in very early spring just as the new leaves are emerging. Small, plumlike fruits slowly ripen as they go from yellow to deep purple. Although edible to humans, the flesh has a bitter aftertaste.

Oso berry is widely scattered on the Mountain, often on the north-facing slopes of steep canyons in open woodlands and chaparral.

BITTER CHERRY   Rose family
Prunus emarginata   Rosaceae

Bitter cherry and the other two prunuses are all uncommon shrubs on Mt. Diablo and are only occasionally encountered. Bitter cherry forms dense, hedgelike growths up to eight feet high with stiff gray branches scribed with circles of lenticels (breathing pores) and has an astringent fragrance on hot days. The small leaves are narrowly wedge shaped and turn yellow before dropping. Clusters of small, white, plumlike flowers appear in early summer followed by tiny, translucent red

Prunus emarginata
BITTER CHERRY,
FLOWERS

"cherries" in late summer or early fall. True to its common name, the flesh is bitter but attractive to birds.

Look for bitter cherry in Pine and Sycamore canyons.

SIERRA PLUM   Rose family
Prunus subcordata   Rosaceae

Sierra plum is a densely branched shrub to six or eight feet high with thorny side branches and oval to broadly elliptical leaves that are finely toothed along their margins. Despite the name *subcordata*, which means partially heart shaped, most leaves show only the faintest sign of being heart shaped

at the base. In late spring, clusters of small, white to pale pink flowers make a brief appearance. These are followed by plumlike, red-purple fruits with a pleasantly sweet flesh.

Prunus subcordata
SIERRA PLUM,
FLOWERING BRANCHES

Sierra plum is quite localized on the Mountain; look for it near Juniper Campground and Deer Flat.

CHOKE CHERRY
Prunus virginiana var. *demissa*

Rose family
Rosaceae

Choke cherry generally grows taller than bitter

cherry and in more discrete clumps. The bark is a brownish red, not particularly fragrant, and the leaves are elliptical with coarsely toothed margins. The showy, plumlike, white flowers are borne in dense spikes beyond the foliage in May or June. Sour, red-purple "cherries" ripen in late summer. They are said to make excellent preserves.

Prunus virginiana demissa
CHOKE CHERRY,
FLOWERS

Uncommon on the Mountain, look for choke cherry near Grape Spring and on Mt. Zion.

CHAPARRAL CURRANT
Ribes malvaceum

Gooseberry family
Grossulariaceae

Chaparral currant is a medium-sized shrub to eight feet high with stiff branches; gray bark; and sticky, fragrant, maple-shaped leaves. It is unusual among shrubs for bursting into flower in the winter, sometimes as early as November. The trusses of nodding flowers are an attractive pale pink purple and are good nectar sources for

Ribes malvaceum
CHAPARRAL CURRANT,
FLOWER TRUSS

bees. Insipid pale purple berries ripen in spring or early summer.

Chaparral currant is frequent in open oak woodlands, canyons, and the edge of chaparral throughout Mt. Diablo.

CANYON GOOSEBERRY
Ribes menziesii

Gosseberry family
Grossulariaceae

Gooseberries differ from currants in having spines and flowers that hide under the leafy branches. Canyon gooseberry features widely arching branches to five or six feet high; rather small, maple-shaped leaves; and triplets of spines at the leaf nodes. The new growth also features softer spines between the leaves. At the end

Ribes menziesii
CANYON GOOSEBERRY,
LEAVES AND FLOWER

of winter, clusters of small, fuchsialike, dark red and white flowers appear, but you need to lift the branches to see them. Extremely spiny, red-purple berries follow. Although birds peck at these berries for food, the berries are difficult to prepare for human consumption.

Canyon gooseberry is occasional in oak woodlands and mixed-evergreen forest on Mt. Diablo.

BLUE WITCH OR BLUE NIGHTSHADE *Solanum umbelliferum*	Nightshade or potato family Solanaceae

Blue witch is more a subshrub than a full-fledged shrub. It has dense, widely spreading, green new stems that form mounded bushes around two feet high. After winter rains, the branches are covered with pale green, narrowly elliptical leaves followed

Solanum umbelliferum
BLUE WITCH, FLOWERING BRANCHES

by massed clusters of saucer-shaped, five-cornered, fragrant, pale blue flowers. Each flower features a conelike central cluster of bright yellow stamens. The berries that follow look like miniature tomatoes and ripen dark purple. Edible to birds, they are considered poisonous to humans. The leaves are often shed during the hot, dry summers, revealing clusters of green twigs.

Blue witch is widespread on the edge of oak woodland and chaparral throughout the Mountain.

SHRUB SNOWBERRY

Honeysuckle family

Symphoricarpos albus var. *laevigatus*

Caprifoliaceae

Shrub snowberry is a small, colonizing shrub to four feet high with pairs of oval to elliptical leaves. Different leaves on the same plant have different patterns—sometimes they're toothed, sometimes

Symphoricarpos albus laevigatus
SNOWBERRY, SHRUB IN FRUIT

lobed on one side, and sometimes entire. Tiny, bell-shaped, pale pink flowers hide under branch tips in late spring. Although the flowers are inconspicuous, the snowy white berries that follow in fall are showy. These spongy berries are insipid but evidently eaten by certain birds.

Shrub snowberry is most common in oak woodlands and riparian forests in canyon bottoms. Wherever these habitats occur, the plant is present.

CREEPING SNOWBERRY

Honeysuckle family

Symphoricarpos mollis

Solanaceae

Creeping snowberry bears many similarities to shrub snowberry, differing mainly in the way it grows. While shrub snowberry has many upright twigs, creeping snowberry grows close to the ground, often skimming the surface of the soil and

Symphoricarpos mollis
CREEPING SNOWBERRY, HABIT OF PLANT

sometimes rooting where a branch is buried. The flowers and fruits are similar to those of the shrub snowberry.

Look for creeping snowberry in dry oak woodlands and other dry woods. It is widespread throughout the Mountain.

EVERGREEN SHRUBS WITH SIMPLE LEAVES

Evergreen shrubs are more numerous than the deciduous kinds, at least in terms of species. This is because most of the drier habitats such as chaparral favor shrubs with long-lasting and thus evergreen leaves. In years of poor rainfall, such shrubs don't need to expend extra water in making a new set of leaves; they make do with last year's set. A common feature of these evergreen shrubs is that the majority also have fragrant oils in their leaves that deter browsers. By evaporating on hot days, they also cool leaf surfaces.

CHAMISE
Adenostoma fasciculatum

Rose family
Rosaceae

Chamise (also known as greasewood) is a densely branched shrub to twelve feet high with thick clusters of narrow, needlelike leaves that look greasy on hot days. The dense panicles of tiny white flowers appear at the beginning of summer. These flowers dry brown as the minute seed pods develop,

Adenostoma fasciculatum
CHAMISE, DETAIL OF FLOWERS

giving the impression from a distance that the shrubs have browned out and lost their leaves.

Chamise is among the most abundant shrubs on the Mountain and dominates large tracts of steep, rocky slopes in the hottest parts of the chaparral.

MOUNT DIABLO MANZANITA
Arctostaphylos auriculata

Heather family
Ericaceae

Arctostaphylos auriculata
MOUNT DIABLO MANZANITA, NEW LEAVES

Mount Diablo manzanita is perhaps the most distinctive of the four species. It is nearly restricted to the Mountain itself. It features clasping, hairy, pale whitish green leaves and pale pink flowers. It is abundant on poor, rocky soils especially near Emmons Canyon and around Knobcone Point.

EASTWOOD MANZANITA
Heather family
Arctostaphylos glandulosa — Ericaceae

Eastwood manzanita is a variable shrub to perhaps ten feet high with narrow, bright green leaves; twigs with sticky hairs (hence *glandulosa*); and clusters of white flowers. Its best distinguishing feature is the burl at the root crown, an expanded woody platform that has dormant buds able to sprout when the branches are injured by fire or by cutting. All the other manzanitas on the Mountain lack these burls, and when seriously injured, are killed outright, unable to resprout.

Eastwood manzanita is occasional on the Mountain. Look for it near Knobcone Point and Emmons Canyon. By contrast, it is widespread elsewhere in much of foothill California.

BIGBERRY MANZANITA
Heather family
Arctostaphylos glauca — Ericaceae

Mount Diablo has four different manzanitas all of which appear similar to the novice. All manzanitas share beautiful, polished, red-purple bark; stiff,

Arctostaphylos glauca
BIGBERRY MANZANITA, LEAVES AND BERRIES

vertically held, ovate leaves; and nodding clusters of small white to pink, urn-shaped flowers that open in winter. The flowers are followed by small, rounded to slightly flattened, reddish, applelike berries that have a mealy flesh. These berries are widely sought for food by a variety of animals and were avidly eaten by the local Indians.

Bigberry manzanita is a tall, treelike shrub to fifteen feet high with pale bluish white leaves of great beauty. The white to palest pink flowers open especially early when winter conditions turn temporarily warm. Unusually large, sticky berries follow. (These berries make an excellent jelly when fully ripe.)

Bigberry manzanita is locally abundant on the Mountain, especially in the Donner Canyon drainage and the area around Murchio Gap and Eagle Peak. It reaches its northernmost distribution here and is a common sight to the south of us.

COMMON MANZANITA
Arctostaphylos manzanita var. *laevigata*

Heather family
Ericaceae

Common manzanita is a very tall, treelike shrub to over fifteen feet high. Older specimens develop impressive trunks that clearly display the gorgeous red-purple bark. The leaves are generally pale green

Arctostaphylos manzanita
COMMON MANZANITA, FLOWERING BRANCHES

to gray green and the white to pale pink flowers are borne abundantly in late January and early February.

Some of the most impressive specimens occur outside the Mountain in adjacent Morgan Territory Regional Preserve. Common manzanita is

A. manzanita
COMMON MANZANITA, TRUNK/BARK

widely scattered in the chaparral on the Mountain, sometimes in company with bigberry manzanita. Look for it in Pine Canyon, Donner Canyon, and Emmons Canyon.

COYOTE BUSH   **Daisy or composite family**
Baccharis pilularis   **Asteraceae**

Coyote bush is a fast-growing, invasive shrub with dense branches, a rounded crown, and numerous, small, bright green, narrowly oval leaves lined with tiny teeth. On warm days, the leaves are pleasantly aromatic. The tiny heads of flowers appear in fall,

Baccharis pilularis
COYOTE BUSH, FLOWERING SHRUBS

the male and female flowers on separate plants. The males feature minute, cream-colored disc flowers that attract bees. The females have snowy white flowers, the white color due to long tufts of hairs that carry the seeds to new homes on the wind.

This opportunistic shrub is the closest thing

we have to a native weedy shrub, invading fields and other disturbed habitats. Many grasslands eventually are covered with coyote bush when grazing and fire are discontinued. Look for coyote bush in open shrublands, oak woodlands, and on the margins of roads and trails.

MULE FAT OR SEEP-WILLOW *Baccharis salicifolia*	Daisy or composite family Asteraceae

Mulefat is another fast-growing shrub but with a different habit and habitat from coyote bush. The

flexible, brownish stems grow long and tall—up to fifteen feet high—with narrow, willowlike, glossy green leaves. Like coyote bush, the male and female flowers appear late in the season, more generally in summer, and occur on separate plants. Both male and female flower heads are whitish to very pale pink and are bee pollinated. Hair-covered seeds follow.

Baccharis salicifolia
MULEFAT, BRANCHES

Mulefat is most abundant in rocky stream courses, where the water lies just beneath the surface. It is widespread on the Mountain especially in the foothills and is common throughout the hotter parts of California.

B. salicifolia
MULEFAT, FLOWER HEADS

BUCKBRUSH
Ceanothus cuneatus

Buckthorn family
Rhamnaceae

Buckbrush is a large, dense, intricately branched shrub to ten feet high with gray bark and pairs

of small, narrowly wedge-shaped, dark green leaves. The undersides have a white, featherlike vein pattern. Masses of tiny, white (occasionally pale purple), fragrant flowers appear in early spring. These are followed by small, three-sided seed pods that split open to shed their seeds.

Ceanothus cuneatus
BUCKBRUSH, SHRUB IN
FULL FLOWER

Buckbrush is among the most abundant shrubs on the Mountain, often growing with chamise (*Adenostoma fasciculatum*). It is found mostly in the chaparral.

JIMBRUSH
Ceanothus oliganthus
var. *sorediatus*

Buckthorn family
Rhamnaceae

Jimbrush is a large, intricately branched shrub or small tree to fifteen feet high with greenish new bark; rigid stems; and elliptical, bright green leaves. The leaves feature three prominent veins that run the length of the leaf. Dense plumes of tiny, pale blue-purple flowers appear in midspring, usually after buckbrush has finished blooming. Three-sided seed pods follow.

Jimbrush is abundant in steep, rocky canyons and hillsides throughout the lower half of the Mountain and is scattered elsewhere. Large specimens have regrown in Back Canyon since the major fire there in 1977.

Ceanothus oliganthus sorediatus
JIMBRUSH, FLOWERING SHRUB

RABBITBRUSH
Chrysothamnus nauseosus

Daisy or composite family
Asteraceae

Rabbitbrush is a small bushy shrub to around three feet high with aromatic, narrow, gray-green leaves. Although the name *nauseosus* suggests an unpleasant odor, most find the odor agreeable. Dense, spikelike clusters of small, bright yellow, rayless flower heads appear in late summer or early fall. The tiny single-seeded fruits are carried on the wind by a tuft of white hairs.

Chrysothamnus nauseosus
RABBITBRUSH, SHRUB IN FULL FLOWER

Rabbitbrush is occasional on the Mountain in hot, dry, exposed sites. Look for it near Emmons Canyon and near the summit. It is most typical of desert environments, conditions sometimes found in the more inhospitable faces of the Mountain such as near the summit.

GOLDEN FLEECE
Ericameria arborescens

Daisy or composite family Asteraceae

Golden fleece is a shrub that often develops one or a few, treelike trunks in age and features shreddy

Ericameria arborescens
GOLDEN FLEECE,
FLOWERING BRANCHES

brown bark. The densely rounded head of branches may be carried up to eight feet high but is typically much less in our area. The linear, bright green leaves are fragrant and look fresh all through the summer drought. Open clusters of bright yellow, usually rayless flower heads open in late summer to be followed by tiny fruits with a tuft of white hairs.

Look for golden fleece in the Emmons Canyon area, at Knobcone Point, and by Murchio Gap.

LINEAR-LEAFED GOLDENBUSH
Ericameria linearifolia

Daisy or composite family Asteraceae

Linear-leafed goldenbush is a small shrub to around two and a half feet high with a much-

Ericameria linearifolia
NARROW-LEAF GOLDENBUSH,
FLOWERING SHRUB

branched crown; many sticky, green, fragrant, linear leaves; and showy, yellow heads of daisylike flowers in early to midspring. The flower heads are reminiscent of garden marguerites. The fruits are similar to other shrubby composites, each tiny, one-seeded ovary carried on wind by a tuft of white hairs.

Linear-leafed goldenbush is widespread and common on the Mountain. It grows on rocky slopes on the edge of chaparral or in open oak woodlands.

YERBA SANTA
Eriodictyon californicum

Waterleaf family
Hydrophyllaceae

Yerba santa is a small shrub to eight feet high with wandering roots that create loose, open colonies. The handsome, broadly lance-shaped, fragrant leaves are shiny and dark green on top, and provided with an intricate white network of veins underneath.

Eriodictyon californicum
YERBA SANTA, LEAFY BRANCHES

Unfortunately, a black sooty mold sometimes disfigures the leaves. Open panicles of white to pale purple, tubular flowers appear in late spring. Butterflies are especially fond of yerba santa nectar. Tiny, two-chambered seed pods follow in summer.

Yerba santa is widespread throughout the chaparral on the Mountain, and prospers best on the edge of taller

E. californicum
YERBA SANTA, FLOWERS

shrubs where it doesn't have to compete with such shrubs as chamise (*Adenostoma fasciculatum*) and buckbrush (*Ceanothus cuneatus*). It moves in opportunistically after fire.

GOLDEN YARROW
Eriophyllum confertiflorum

Daisy or composite family
Asteraceae

Golden yarrow is a subshrub to around a foot high with many branches. The small leaves are evergreen

except in the hottest summers, when they're reduced in size or partially lost. Each narrow leaf is deeply pinnately lobed, dull gray green on top and covered with woolly, white hairs underneath. The small, bright yellow, daisylike flower heads are borne in flat-topped clusters in late spring and early summer. Although called a yarrow, the true yarrows (*Achillea* spp.) are only distantly related.

Eriophyllum confertiflorum
GOLDEN YARROW,
FLOWERING SHRUB WITH
POLLINATING NATIVE BEES

Golden yarrow is widespread on the Mountain on rocky outcrops near the edge of chaparral and coastal sage scrub.

COAST SILK TASSEL BUSH
Garrya elliptica

Garrya family
Garryaceae

The silk tassel bushes are closely related and sometimes confusing to sort out. The coast silk tassel grows taller, sometimes up to fifteen feet high, and features pairs of large oval leaves that are dark green on top, wavy along the edges, and whitish underneath. The shrubs are male or female and bloom in the dead of winter. The male shrubs feature long, dangling chains (catkins) of gray-green flowers with long stamens, while the female shrubs have somewhat shorter catkins of flowers. After wind has carried the pollen, the female catkins plump out and develop into what looks like a chain of small gray grapes. Each fruit has red-purple flesh inside.

Coast silk tassel is occasional near Knobcone Point and in Dan Cook Canyon.

Garrya elliptica
COAST SILK TASSEL,
MALE CATKINS

GREEN-LEAF SILK TASSEL BUSH
Garrya fremontii

Garrya family
Garryaceae

Green-leaf silk tassel bush is a smaller shrub than coast silk tassel, seldom growing over six feet high with pairs of oval, bright green leaves (both surfaces) that strongly resemble manzanita leaves. (Of course, manzanitas have red bark and alternate leaves.) The male and female catkins are similar to the coast silk tassel except, perhaps, they're a bit shorter.

Garrya fremontii
GREENLEAF SILK TASSEL,
LEAVES AND MALE CATKINS

Green-leaf silk tassel is uncommon in our area and needs to be carefully sought out. It is most characteristic of chaparral in the upper parts of the Mountain such as at Juniper Campground and near the summit of the Mountain.

MATCHSTICK
Gutierrezia californica

Daisy or composite family Asteraceae

Matchstick is best described as a shrublet—woody only at the base—growing around a foot tall with open, multiple green branches that create a delicate green filagree. The tiny, scalelike to linear leaves are of the same bright green hue. Miniature yellow heads of daisylike flowers don't appear until late

Gutierrezia sp.
MATCHSTICK, SHRUB IN FULL FLOWER

summer and may continue into early fall.

Out of flower, matchstick is seldom noticed and is probably more common than would be suspected. Nonetheless, it is restricted mainly to rock outcrops low in nutrients, where it avoids competition with bigger shrubs. Look for it in the Knobcone Point area.

TOYON OR CALIFORNIA HOLLY
Heteromeles arbutifolia

Rose family Rosaceae

Toyon is a versatile shrub that may grow low and dense where exposed to rocky soils and drought

Heteromeles arbutifolia
TOYON, FRUITING BRANCHES

or into a small tree in the partial shade of woodlands. The bark is dark grayish brown, and the leaves are large, narrowly elliptical, leathery, and lined with coarse teeth. The rounded clusters of small white flowers appear in midsummer. They are followed in fall by masses of bright red berries attractive to birds. Although edible to humans, these berries are seldom tasty enough to bother with.

Toyon is widespread on the Mountain in several habitats including chaparral, oak woodland, and even mixed-evergreen forest.

RED ROCK PENSTEMON
Keckiella corymbosa

Snapdragon family
Scrophulariaceae

Red rock penstemon is a shrublet with dense, low, often prostrate branches that reach only a foot or so high. Pairs of small, glossy, rounded leaves are attractive year round. Racemes of showy, highly irregular, two-lipped, scarlet flowers appear in summer. Two-chambered seed pods follow. The flowers are a strong draw to hummingbirds.

Keckiella corymbosa
RED ROCK PENSTEMON, DETAIL OF FLOWERS

Red rock penstemon is restricted to rocky outcrops on the tops of promontories, where its roots penetrate deeply into fissures. The Mary Bowerman Trail near the summit of the Mountain is a good place to see it.

PITCHERSAGE
Lepechinia calycina

Mint family
Lamiaceae

Pitchersage is a small shrub, woody at the base, with many, widely spreading, arching branches. The

large, highly fragrant leaves are oval-triangular, gray green, and wrinkled on the surface. Hanging racemes of large, bell-shaped, irregular, white or pale purple flowers appear in late spring and early summer. After the blossoms finish, the net-veined sepals enlarge into pitcher-shaped receptacles that contain four large, one-seeded fruits.

Lepechinia calycina
PITCHER SAGE, LEAVES
AND OLD SPENT FLOWERS

Pitchersage is frequent on rocky slopes near the edge of chaparral (trailsides, for example) and coastal sage scrub. It is abundant after fire.

WAND BUSH MALLOW
Malacothamnus fasciculatus

Mallow family
Malvaceae

The bush mallows are fast-growing shrubs that seldom persist more than a few years. Wand bush

mallow has several varieties, most of which grow tall and slender, but our local version grows as a three- to four-foot-tall

Malacothamnus fasciculatus
WAND BUSH MALLOW,
FLOWERING BRANCHES

shrub with widely arching branches. The rounded, slightly lobed leaves are gray-green and covered with felted hairs to reduce water loss. Wandlike clusters of showy, pink-purple, cup-shaped flowers appear in mid to late spring and put on a brief but impressive show.

Wand bush mallow occurs in just a few sites on the Mountain. It would doubtless be much more abundant after fire, as it tends to be a fire follower, and often the plants die out after a few years from competition with taller shrubs. A couple of stands occur just inside the Park boundary on the North Gate Road.

FREMONT BUSH MALLOW   Mallow family
Malacothamnus fremontii   Malvaceae

Fremont bush mallow is much like the wand bush mallow but has stiffer, more upright branches, almost unlobed leaves, and a dense covering of a silvery-white felt from numerous hairs. The blossoms are also similar to the wand bush mallow.

Fremont bush mallow may appear in large numbers after a burn in the chaparral but, like its sister species, declines after a few years. The best places to seek it out are on barren rocky hills where other shrubs haven't taken over. An impressive

Malacothamnus fremontii
FREMONT BUSH MALLOW,
HABIT OF PLANT

stand occurs on the Summit Trail just above the Devil's Elbow as well as at a bend along Globe Lily Trail. It is also occasional in the Mitchell Canyon area.

STICKY OR BUSH MONKEYFLOWER
Mimulus aurantiacus

Snapdragon family
Scrophulariaceae

Bush monkeyflower is a small shrub to two or three feet high with pairs of narrowly lance-shaped leaves that are sticky to the touch on hot

days. (This stickiness cuts down on water loss.) The clusters of orange flowers are highly ornamental and are two-lipped with a patch of darker orange on the lower lip providing a nectar guide to visiting bees. The flowers open from midspring into early summer; two-chambered seed pods follow.

Mimulus aurantiacus
BUSH MONKEYFLOWER,
FLOWERING BRANCHES

Bush monkeyflower is common in a variety of habitats on the Mountain including open oak woodlands, the edge of chaparral, and coastal sage scrub. It prefers areas where larger shrubs don't crowd it out.

SCRUB OAK
Quercus berberidifolia

Oak or beech family
Fagaceae

Scrub oak is so named because it forms a dense, evergreen shrub rather than growing as a massively trunked tree. The intricate branches are rigid and stiff and covered with tough, elliptical, dark green leaves lined with prickly teeth and often curled under along the margins. The undersides are often pale and whitish.

Like other oaks, the male flowers are in narrow, hanging, yellow catkins, and the female flowers appear in ones and twos between the new leaves

Quercus berberidifolia
SCRUB OAK, SHRUB LOADED WITH MALE CATKINS

and stems. The ripe acorns sit in a warty cup and are plump and rounded.

Scrub oak or its equivalents have given chaparral its name (this Spanish word means *grove of scrub oaks*). It is a frequent component of chaparral on steep rocky slopes but seldom occurs in the large stands that chamise (*Adenostoma fasciculatum*) and buckbrush (*Ceanothus cuneatus*) do. A good place to see it is on the Mary Bowerman Trail (formerly named the Fire Interpretive Trail) near the summit.

LEATHER OAK	Oak or beech family
Quercus durata	Fagaceae

Leather oak is a second but less common species of scrub oak. In its branching pattern and height it is similar to the common scrub oak but the leaves are often strongly curled under and look dusty on the top. (A good hand lens reveals masses of tiny, starburstlike

Quercus durata
LEATHER OAK, CLOSE UP OF LEAVES AND ACORN

hairs.) Male catkins, female flowers, and acorns resemble the scrub oak and occasionally the two species hybridize.

Leather oak is rather uncommon on the Mountain and is restricted to just a few sites, where soils are unusually thin and low in nutrients. In most areas, it is restricted to serpentine-derived soils, but serpentine is uncommon on the Mountain and so it sometimes grows on other similarly difficult soils. Look for it near the top of Murchio Gap.

COFFEE BERRY	**Buckthorn family**
Rhamnus californica	**Rhamnaceae**

Rhamnus californica
COFFEE BERRY, LEAVES AND RIPENING FRUITS

Coffee berry is a much branched shrub to ten feet high with glossy green, narrowly elliptical leaves to four inches long lined with minute teeth. One of the best identifying traits is the arching side veins which swoop out but don't quite touch the leaf edge. Clusters of tiny, star-shaped, pale yellow flowers appear in late spring and attract bees. The fruits gradually turn from lime green to yellow, red, and finally dark purple. The coffeelike seeds inside are not edible.

Coffee berry is widely scattered throughout the Mountain both in oak woodland and chaparral.

HOLLY-LEAF REDBERRY
Rhamnus ilicifolia

Buckthorn family
Rhamnaceae

Rhamnus ilicifolia
HOLLY-LEAF REDBERRY, FLOWERING BRANCHES

Holly-leaf redberry is a stiffly branched, upright shrub to twelve feet high with small, glossy, dark green, curled leaves edged with prickly teeth. Although related to coffee berry, the leaves are much smaller and initially don't give the impression of a close relationship. But the clusters of tiny, yellow-green, starlike flowers

R. ilicifolia
HOLLY-LEAF REDBERRY,
FLOWERING BRANCH

are similar. The small, one-seeded fruits that follow ripen bright red on plants with female flowers; male plants produce no fruits. Birds are attracted by the bright colors of the fruits, which for humans are a strong laxative.

Holly-leaf redberry is widely scattered but seldom found in large numbers. It occurs in oak woodland and on the edge of chaparral and is a common sight in Mitchell Canyon.

BLACK SAGE
Salvia mellifera

Mint family
Lamiaceae

Salvia mellifera
BLACK SAGE, SHRUB IN FLOWER

Black sage is a small shrub to perhaps five feet high with pairs of dark green, narrowly spoon-shaped leaves that are wrinkled on their upper surface. Small, white to pale purple, two-lipped flowers are arranged in circles in narrow spikes. Bees are especially fond of their nectar. Tiny, one-seeded fruits develop inside the flowers' sepals. It is not obvious why this sage is called *black* but perhaps it's because the shrubs appear dark from a distance.

Black sage is abundant on steep, rocky, shallow soils throughout the Mountain. Together with California sagebrush (*Artemisia californica*), it dominates wide swaths of coastal sage scrub and also often grows with chamise (*Adenostoma fasciculatum*).

The Mt. Diablo region is large and varied; it embraces numerous trails and sites to visit. Whether you're out for a drive and simply want to stop along the road to look at plants or you're up for a day-long hike, you're likely to see a great variety of shrubs and trees. The following section is a short synopsis of my favorite places to visit. It is not intended to be comprehensive or all inclusive.

WITHIN MT. DIABLO STATE PARK

ROADS

The two major paved roads on the Mountain are the North Gate and South Gate roads, which join about midway up the Mountain at the Junction Ranger Station. The road to the top at this junction is Summit Road.

To reach North Gate Road, from Hwy. 680 in Walnut Creek, take the Ygnacio Valley Road off-ramp. Follow Ygnacio Valley Road east to Walnut Avenue. Turn right on Walnut Avenue and follow it to Oak Grove Road; again turn right on it for a very short distance to North Gate Road; take a left, which leads into the Park.

For South Gate Road, from Hwy. 680 in Danville, take the El Cerro Blvd. off-ramp. Drive east to the junction of Diablo Road Continue straight ahead on Diablo Road to Mt. Diablo Scenic Blvd., which becomes South Gate Road leading into the Park.

FOR NORTH GATE ROAD: There is only a handful of well marked pull-outs and only one or two places with trail access. The road starts in rolling grassy hills, then enters steep hills covered mostly with oak or foothill woodland. Prominent trees along the road include blue oak, coast live oak, canyon live oak, California buckeye, and gray pine. A couple of rare occurrences of the wand bush mallow also occur on this road.

FOR SOUTH GATE ROAD: two interesting
stops given in the order you encounter them as you
drive up South Gate Road:

• ROCK CITY
This wonderland of rocks is home to a varied oak
woodland with blue oak, California black oak, interior
live oak, and others. There are several trails through
here including the Fossil Ridge Road, the Summit Trail
(a great trail to follow all the way to the top of the
Mountain), and the Wall Point Road.

• CURRY POINT
The pull-out for the road to Knobcone Point. Follow
Knobcone Point Road directly down to Knobcone
Point. En route you pass through oak woodland and
gray pines, then come to rocky slopes with chaparral
including toyon, Mt. Diablo manzanita, and silk tassel
bush along with knobcone pines.

FOR SUMMIT ROAD (above the intersection
of South and North Gate roads.) The stops are given
in order from the bottom to the top:

• JUNIPER CAMPGROUND
This popular campground is home to many beautiful
shrubs including hopbush, pitcher sage, Sierra plum,
and manzanitas and is also an excellent place to see
California junipers. You can take several trails from
here, among them the Deer Flat Road down to Deer
Flat, and Juniper Trail, which takes you to the top of
the Mountain.

• DEVILS ELBOW
This sharp bend in the road is where you intersect the
Summit Trail at a point above Juniper Campground.
You can access the North Peak Trail here, which winds
down to Prospectors Gap, then goes steeply up North
Peak Road to the Mountain's seldom-visited North
Peak.

• PARKING LOT FOR THE MARY BOWERMAN TRAIL *(formerly named the Fire Interpretive Trail)* just below the summit of the Mountain. This area is home to chaparral and dense low forests of interior live oak and canyon live oak.

THREE OTHER ACCESS ROADS TO THE PARK:

• MITCHELL CANYON ROAD out of Clayton takes you to a large parking lot and small visitor's center. Several trails depart from here, including one of the best short hikes on the Mountain up Mitchell Canyon. You can also hike up Eagle Peak or hike across the foothills to Back Canyon and make a large loop hike. Mitchell Canyon features oak and foothill woodlands including Coulter pines, chaparral, and a fine example of riparian woodland with bigleaf maple, white alder, Fremont cottonwood, and California bay.

• REGENCY DRIVE off Clayton Road in east Clayton dead ends by a promontory overlooking the start of Donner Canyon. Trails lead into Donner and Back canyons through oak and foothill woodlands.

• GREEN VALLEY ROAD (a turnoff from Diablo Road in Danville) ends at Macedo Ranch. Although this area is not particularly inspiring, you can take Wall Point Road to Emmons Canyon Road, continue on Wall Point Road, or go to Stage Road, all good hikes with interesting shrubs and trees.

HIKES

Hikes on the Mountain vary from easy and short such as the Mary Bowerman Trail (.8 mile long) to long and demanding. It's a feasible but strenuous hike to the top of the Mountain from such put-in points as Mitchell Canyon and Donner Canyon. Hikes are best done in the spring, midfall, and winter (although trails become incredibly muddy in foothill meadows after rains). Summer is often exeedingly hot, dry, and dehydrating. Be sure to carry a good trail map with you and carry plenty of water.

FALLS TRAIL

From Regency Drive, hike up Donner Canyon Road to Cardinet Oaks Road, turn left and follow Cardinet Oaks Road to the junction with the Falls Trail. Return by making a loop via Middle Trail to rejoin Donner Canyon Road. The loop passes several beautiful cascades (winter and early spring are best). Trees include various oaks, gray pine, Coulter pine (limited), California buckeye, and white alders. Shrubs include flowering ash, bigberry manzanita, buckbrush and jimbrush, toyon, linear-leaved goldenbush, and more.

LOOP FROM DONNER CANYON TO BACK CANYON

Hike up Donner Canyon Road from Regency Drive to the intersection with the Tick Wood Trail. Turn right and follow this trail over a ridge and steeply down into Back Canyon. Turn right again and follow Back Canyon Trail which becomes Back Creek Road, ending back at Regency Drive. This is a beautiful hike for spring wildflowers and includes a good measure of oak and foothill woodlands, limited riparian woodland, chaparral, and coastal sage scrub. One of the uncommon shrubs on this stretch is the flowering ash.

MITCHELL CANYON

You can hike up the road that follows Mitchell Canyon for around 2 miles before the trail leaves the canyon and ascends steeply. This easy walk is especially fine in the spring and fall. Vines include California grape, riparian clematis, and vine honeysuckle. Riparian trees include California bay, white alder, bigleaf maple, Fremont cottonwood, and northern black walnut. Shrubs include blue witch, chamise, hollyleaf redberry, coffee berry, pitcher sage, black sage, chaparral currant, squawbush, and poison oak.

DEER FLAT LOOP

If you're up for a moderately strenuous hike of around 8 miles, this is one of the best. From Mitchell Canyon, continue steeply uphill to Deer Flat for fabulous views. From Deer Flat, take the Meridian Ridge Road to

Murchio Gap, and turn left onto the Back Creek Trail down into Back Canyon. At the mouth of Back Canyon, turn left to find the Coulter Pine Trail, which will bring you back to the Mitchell Canyon parking lot. This hike takes you through a wide variety of terrain and plant communities including riparian woodland, Coulter pine forest, foothill and oak woodland, grassland, chaparral, and coastal sage scrub.

• EAGLE PEAK

Another moderately strenuous hike. You can ascend by a short front route from two directions (Mitchell or Back canyons) or make a long loop. For one route up the front way, hike up Back Canyon a short ways, turn right onto the Coulter Pine Trail for a short ways, then go left onto a switchback trail to the shoulder of Eagle Peak. When you reach the shoulder, turn left onto the main Eagle Peak trail and continue to the summit for grand, sweeping views. If you wish to make a loop, you can continue from the summit to Murchio Gap, turn right and walk down to Deer Flat, and return down Mitchell Canyon and then return to Back Canyon on the Coulter Pine Trail. As with the Deer Flat loop, you'll pass through most of the major plant communities on the Mountain.

• MARY BOWERMAN TRAIL: *(formerly named the Fire Intepretive Trail).*

This easy, .8 mile loop starts at the parking lot just below the summit. The trail takes you through oak woodland, chaparral, coastal sage scrub, and rock outcroppings. Late spring is an excellent time to visit although the red rock penstemon doesn't bloom until June or July. Other shrubs include yerba santa, toyon, hollyleaf redberry, coffee berry, golden yarrow, mountain mahogany, pitcher sage, and black sage.

• LOOP FROM JUNIPER CAMPGROUND TO THE SUMMIT:

To make a pleasant and relatively short loop, park at Juniper Campground and follow the Juniper Trail downhill, cross Summit Road, and join Summit Trail up to the top of the Mountain. You go through oak woodland and chaparral and pass a dense stand of the uncommon Fremont bush mallow en route. If you want a bit of additional walking, take the short and easy Mary Bowerman Trail, then head back down to Juniper Campground on the Juniper Trail.

● WALL POINT ROAD LOOP WITH A SIDE EXCURSION TO EMMONS CANYON

From Macedo Ranch, follow Wall Point Road to the intersection with Emmons Canyon Road and turn right onto the latter, and walk a short way. This area is of interest to ecologists because of the influence of fire; the chaparral in this area is in various stages from mature, undisturbed stands to relatively young shrubs recovering from fire. Double back to intersection with Wall Point Road. Turn right and follow it to Secret Trail. Follow it to Barbeque Terrace Road. Turn left and follow it to Stage Road. Turn left and follow it to Dusty Road, then turn left again and follow it to Wall Point Road. Turn left to return to Macedo Ranch.

OUTSIDE THE STATE PARK BOUNDARIES

There are several adjacent areas to the Park that are very much worth a visit. They vary in size but most have at least several trails.

● DIABLO FOOTHILLS REGIONAL PARK AND PINE CANYON

In Walnut Creek, turn right onto Walnut Avenue from Ygnacio Valley Road; turn right onto Castle Rock Road and follow it to the end. You park next to Castle Rock Regional Recreation Area and follow the road into Diablo Foothills Regional Park. You can then walk through Pine Canyon, while enjoying views of the castlelike rocks on the left and the shade of a mixed-evergreen forest. The road leaves the forest at the end by Pine Pond in Mt. Diablo State Park. Or you can take several roads uphill along Pine Canyon to

Briones- Mt.Diablo Trail, which comes into Wall Point Road. Long or short loops are possible using this basic pattern. The area is full of wildflowers in the spring.

• MARSH CREEK AND MORGAN TERRITORY ROADS

Both roads lie to the east of Mt. Diablo and feature beautiful riparian corridors with such trees as Fremont cottonwood, western sycamore, bigleaf maple, and white alder. In addition, there is extensive mixed oak forest and woodland.

• MORGAN TERRITORY REGIONAL PRESERVE

This regional park lies to the southeast of Mt. Diablo. For many, the easiest access to the main parking area is from Livermore; from Hwy 580, take the North Livermore Avenue exit, turn left and drive a few miles to Morgan Territory Road and turn right. The main parking lot is around 5 miles north of this intersection. The park features many fine hiking trails that take you through oak woodland, riparian woodland, and chaparral. This is an excellent place to see a wide variety of oaks including coast live oak, interior live oak, canyon live oak, blue oak, valley oak, and California black oak.

Websites, botanical gardens, and books are all excellent resources for learning more about trees and shrubs. While few are devoted exclusively to Mount Diablo, many have useful information that may help in identification, naming, and ecology.

• BOTANIC GARDENS & ARBORETA •

- Regional Parks Botanic Garden
**Intersection South Park Dr. & Wildcat Canyon
Rd., Tilden Park, Berkeley, CA 94708
nativeplants.org
Open 8:30 am – 5 pm daily**
This garden has collections from all over the state and features a majority of the trees and shrubs found on Mount Diablo.

- San Francisco Botanical Garden at
Strybing Arboretum
**9th Avenue at Lincoln Way, San Francisco,
CA 94122 • 415-661-1316 • strybing.org
Open M-F 8 am – 4:30 pm; weekends
10 am – 5 pm**
This garden features a large section devoted to California natives. Several of the trees and many of the shrubs from the Mountain grow here.

- UC Berkeley Botanical Garden
**200 Centennial Drive, Berkeley, CA 94720
415-642-3343 • mip.berkeley.edu/garden
Open 9 am – 5 pm Sept thru May and until
7 pm Memorial Day to Labor Day
Admission $3; additional parking charge**
A large section on California natives features many shrubs and trees described in this book.

• WEBSITES •

- **calflora.net** Informative, photographic website of California natives and useful for its meanings of scientific names.

- **nativeplants.org** *Friends* of Regional Parks Botanic Garden. Find out about classes, events, and pertinent information on this website.

- **cnps.org** California Native Plant Society

- **ebcnps.org** East Bay Chapter CNPS. The Society sponsors free field trips and has evening lectures on native plants.

- **calflora.org** CalFlora Database, a collection of data and 20,000 photos of 8,375 vascular plants of California.

- **calphoto.com/wflowers.htm** California Wildflower Hotsheet.

- **calypteanna.com/ca-natives.htm** California Native Plants Discussion Group.

- **mdia.org** Mount Diablo Interpretive Association, instrumental in education about preserving the Mountain.

• BOOKS •

Bakker, Elna. *An Island Called California*. UC Press, 1984. Relates plant communities, habitats, and geography in a transect across California. Highly recommended.

Ertter. Barbara and Mary L. Bowerman. *The Flowering Plants and Ferns of Mount Diablo, California*. CNPS. 2002

Hickman, James C. ed. *The Jepson Manual*. UC Press, 1993. The "bible" for identifying wild plants in California.

Keator, Glenn. *Introduction to Trees of the San Francisco Bay Region*. UC Press, 2002. Trees that occur naturally in the nine-county Bay Area.

Keator, Glenn. *The Life of an Oak: An Intimate Portrait*. Heyday Books, 1998. Provides a description of this important local genus on a worldwide basis.

Lanner, Ron. *Conifers of California*. Cachuma Press, 1999. The best book on native conifers. Excellent color paintings and photographs.

Pavlik, Muick, Johnson, and Popper. *Oaks of California*. 1993. A beautiful overview of our many species of native oaks including identification, ecology, preservation, and more.

Stuart, John & John Sawyer. *The Trees and Shrubs of California*. UC Press, 2001. A good basic book for identifying native trees and a large number of native shrubs.

GLOSSARY OF TERMS

ALTERNATE • Leaves are attached singly at each point along the stem.

BRACT • A modified leaf associated with flowers. Bracts are often like smaller versions of ordinary vegetative leaves.

CATKIN • Chains of tiny, petalless, wind-pollinated flowers typical of willows, alders, silk tassel bushes, and others.

CHAPARRAL • Stands of drought-tolerant, mostly evergreen shrubs that favor hot, steep, rocky hillsides.

COASTAL SAGE SCRUB • Stands of small, often fragrant, sometimes summer-deciduous shrubs that grow in similar situations to chaparral. Coastal sage scrub often temporarily replaces the larger chaparral shrubs after fire.

COMPOUND • Leaves that are divided into two or more separate leaflets. Compound leaves generally have a bud at the base where they attach to the stem but not at the base of the individual leaflets.

CONIFER • Trees and shrubs with scalelike or needlelike leaves that bear their seeds in cones. Conifers do not have flowers.

DECIDUOUS • Shrubs and trees that lose all of their leaves part of the year. Most of our shrubs and trees are winter deciduous, but a few are summer deciduous.

DIOECIOUS • Where male and female flowers are borne on separate plants. Examples: willows and cottonwoods.

DISC FLOWER • The tiny flowers in the center of a daisy or aster. These flowers produce nectar and later seeds, while the petal-like ray flowers that surround them are mainly for show.

DRUPE • A fleshy fruit with a single, hard seed. Examples: peaches, plums, and avocados.

EVERGREEN • Shrubs and trees that retain some leaves throughout the year.

HERBACEOUS • Plants that don't develop wood or bark.

LEAFLET • The parts of a compound leaf.

LENTICEL • The breathing pores found in the new bark of shrubs and trees. Lenticels often appear as small dots or lines.

LOBED • Leaves whose margins are clearly indented. Lobes may be shallow as in blue oak leaves or deep as in valley oak leaves.

OPPOSITE • Leaves arranged in pairs on the stem.

OVARY • The bottom part of the pistil of a flower. The ovary looks like a small green sac and contains the future seeds. When the ovary has ripened, it becomes a fruit.

PALMATE • Pattern of leaves, lobes, or veins that mimic the fingers on a hand.

PANICLE • Much-branched clusters of flowers. The main stalk carries several side branches and each of these side branches is rebranched.

PETAL • The (usually) colorful part of a flower. The petals are normally the most obvious feature of a flower and lie just inside the sepals.

PINNATE • Pattern of leaves, lobes, or veins that resembles the parts of a feather.

POLLEN • The (usually) yellow dust that issues from stamens.

POLLINATION • The process of moving the pollen from a stamen to a stigma of a flower. Most flowers are designed to attract insects or birds, which accomplish cross-pollination by making repeated visits to different flowers on different plants.

RACEME • Flower arrangement where a long stalk carries several side branches, each with a flower.

RAY • The petal-like flowers around the edge of a daisy or other members of the composite family (Asteraceae). The petals of ray flowers are long, flattened, and tongue shaped.

RIPARIAN • Vegetation that occurs along permanent water courses.

SAMARA • The winged fruits of trees such as maples, ashes, and hopbush. The wings help move the fruits by wind.

SCALE • Tiny, fish-scale-shaped leaves typical of such conifers as junipers.

SEMIEVERGREEN • Leaves that drop when conditions are especially cold in winter or especially dry in summer.

SEPAL • The outermost part of a typical flower and usually green. The sepals protect the inner parts of the flower while in bud.

SEROTINOUS • Seed cones whose scales are glued shut, generally opening only after the heat of a fire dries up the glue.

SERPENTINE • Smooth bluish or greenish rocks that are high in magnesium and iron, but otherwise form a nutrient-poor soil, which is difficult for most plants to grow in.

SIMPLE • Leaves that are not compound but in one piece. (They may be lobed.)

SPIKE • A narrow cluster of flowers borne directly along a stalk.

SPUR SHOOT • Tiny nubbinlike stems that bear leaves or flowers. Spur shoots are typical of pines and apple trees. (The fruits of apples always appear on spur shoots.)

STAMEN • The male part of a flower, which consists of a stalk (filament) and sac (anther). The anther produces millions of minute pollen grains.

STIGMA • The sticky or hairy end of the pistil (female part) of a flower. A pistil consists of an ovary at the base, a stalklike style, and a stigma.

STIPULES • Pairs of (usually) tiny appendages at the base of leaves. Stipules are typical of leaves in the pea and rose families but are missing in many other families.

STYLE • The stalk at the top of the ovary in a flower's pistil. The end of the style is enlarged into a stigma, which receives the pollen.

SUBSHRUB • A usually small bushy plant that is woody only at the base.

TENDRIL • Curled stalks or ends of leaves that allow vines to cling to shrubs and trees as they climb.

TRIFOLIATE • Compound leaves divided into three leaflets. Examples: poison oak, squaw bush, and hopbush.

TWO-LIPPED • Tubular flowers whose petal lobes are irregular and arranged in two sets: the upper set of two petal lobes is generally shorter while the lower set of three petal lobes is often larger.

VINE • Plants that climb other plants for support in order to reach the sun. Some vines are woody and included in this book; others are nonwoody or herbaceous. Examples of woody vines: California grape and virgin's bower.